GRASSES

VERSATILE PARTNERS FOR UNCOMMON GARDEN DESIGN

GRASSES

NANCY J. ONDRA

PHOTOGRAPHY BY SAXON HOLT

 Storey Books
North Adams,
Massachusetts

*The mission of Storey Publishing is to serve our customers
by publishing practical information that encourages personal
independence in harmony with the environment.*

Edited by Gwen W. Steege and
Marie A. Salter

Art direction by Cindy McFarland and
Wendy Palitz

Cover and text design by Cindy McFarland
based on a design by Josh Chen of Chen
Design

Text production by Erin Lincourt

Illustrations by Bobbi Angell (pages 11,
12, 14, and 15) and Elayne Sears (pages
24, 26, 28, and 29), and garden plan keys
by Alison Kolesar

Indexed by Susan Olason, Indexes &
Knowledge Maps

front cover: 'Morning Light' miscanthus
(*Miscanthus sinensis* 'Morning Light')

front flap: 'Siskiyou Blue' Idaho fescue
(*Festuca idahoensis* 'Siskiyou Blue')

back cover: purple fountain grass (*Pennisetum setaceum* 'Rubrum') and Mexican
feather grass *(Nassella tenuissima)*

back flap: giant feather grass *(Stipa
gigantea)*

page 2: giant feather grass *(Stipa gigantea)*
and ruby grass *(Rhynchelytrum nerviglume)*

page 5: giant feather grass *(Stipa gigantea)*

page 6 (left to right): purple fountain
grass *(Pennisetum setaceum* 'Rubrum'),
great drooping sedge *(Carex pendula),*
perennial quaking grass *(Briza media)*

page 7: giant feather grass *(Stipa gigantea)*

Text copyright © 2002 by Nancy J. Ondra
Photographs copyright © 2002 by Saxon Holt
(see page 135 for garden, location, and design credits)

Storey Books are available for special premium and promotional uses and for customized
editions. For further information, please call Storey's Custom Publishing Department at
1-800-793-9396.

Printed in China by C & C Offset Printing Co., Ltd.
10 9 8 7 6 5 4 3 2 1

Library of Congress Cataloging-in-Publication Data

Ondra, Nancy J.
    Grasses : versatile partners for uncommon garden design / by Nancy J. Ondra.
        p. cm.
    Includes index.
    ISBN 1-58017-423-X (alk. paper)
    1. Ornamental grasses. I. Title.

    SB431.7 .O54 2002
    635.9'349—dc21

                                                            2001049845

To Mom and Dad, Gwennie, Princess, Ouija, and Uncle Lucky —
thanks for being there!

CONTENTS

VERSATILE PARTNERS

ABOVE: A vibrant threesome of Bowles' golden sedge (*Carex elata* 'Aurea'), *Hosta* 'Janet', and a cherry-pink *Astilbe* would brighten any garden.

OPPOSITE: Like a bright sentry at the gateway, 'Cosmopolitan' miscanthus (*Miscanthus sinensis* var. *condensatus* 'Cosmopolitan') is a graceful partner for climbing roses ('Complicata') and other vines.

What would you give for a plant that boasts not only handsome foliage and charming flowers, but also eye-catching fall color and showy seed heads that make your garden a visual delight for many months every year? You are about to discover that ideal plant in the fascinating world of ornamental grasses. These versatile plants come in all sizes, from ground-huggers to shrub-size clumps, and in many forms, from upright tufts to mop-top mounds and arching fountains. They easily adapt to the same conditions most garden plants thrive in, rarely needing any special soil preparation or maintenance. And more subtly, their gentle movement and soft whispering sounds can bring your garden alive as no other plants do.

You may have heard gardeners worry that grasses look weedy, take over a garden, and are just not very interesting. But these complaints simply don't hold up. You certainly couldn't say that the flowing mounds of golden Hakone grass (*Hakonechloa macra* 'Aureola') or the dramatic fountainlike form of Japanese silver grass *(Miscanthus sinensis)* looks like weeds. It's true that some grasses can spread (and fast), but so do many popular perennials, and you can take measures to control them in return for their beauty.

The most delightful features of grasses — and their real value for garden design — become apparent when they are partnered with other garden plants. Through the ideas and images on these pages, I hope you will be inspired to take full advantage of these uniquely appealing plants.

What Is a Grass?

It doesn't take a degree in botany to be able to grow and enjoy ornamental grasses. But it does help to be familiar with the terms that describe the basic features of these plants — their flower forms, plant shapes, growth habits — so you can understand their descriptions and make well-informed decisions about which grasses to try.

Not all plants called ornamental grasses are actually "true" grasses. *True grasses* are in the Poaceae family (also known as Gramineae) and include lawn grasses, cereal grains, and the showier species grown as ornamental garden plants, as well as bamboo. But the term *grass* has also become a convenient way to identify a range of plants that share a similar trait: namely, narrow to straplike leaves. This group commonly includes not only true grasses, but also sedges, rushes, and cattails. Some common examples of narrow-leaved perennials grown primarily for their foliage include liriopes (*Liriope* spp.), sedges (such as Bowles' golden sedge [*Carex elata* 'Aurea']), and New Zealand flax *(Phormium tenax)*.

An old garden rhyme offers some hints that may help you keep all of these plants straight: "Sedges have edges and rushes are round; grasses are hollow and rush all around." For a more scientific approach, study the illustrations at the right and compare flowering structures to make an accurate identification.

Variegated feather reed grass (*Calamagrostis* x *acutiflora* 'Overdam') shares a perennial border with peonies and *Eupatorium*.

SEDGES HAVE EDGES . . .

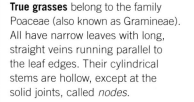

Poa spp.

Typha spp.

Juncus spp.

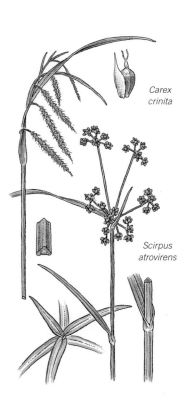

Carex crinita

Scirpus atrovirens

True grasses belong to the family Poaceae (also known as Gramineae). All have narrow leaves with long, straight veins running parallel to the leaf edges. Their cylindrical stems are hollow, except at the solid joints, called *nodes*.

Cattails are aquatic or marginal plants in the family Typhaceae. They have flat, narrow, irislike leaves and distinctive velvety-brown, cigar-shaped flowering structures. Their stems are solid.

Rushes are grasslike plants that belong to the family Juncaceae. The stems of rushes are typically cylindrical, like those of true grasses, but they tend to be solid rather than hollow and lack the nodes grasses have.

Sedges, in the family Cyperaceae, also lack nodes and have solid stems, but their stems are not cylindrical; instead, they are normally three-angled (in other words, triangular in cross-section).

FLOWER FORMS

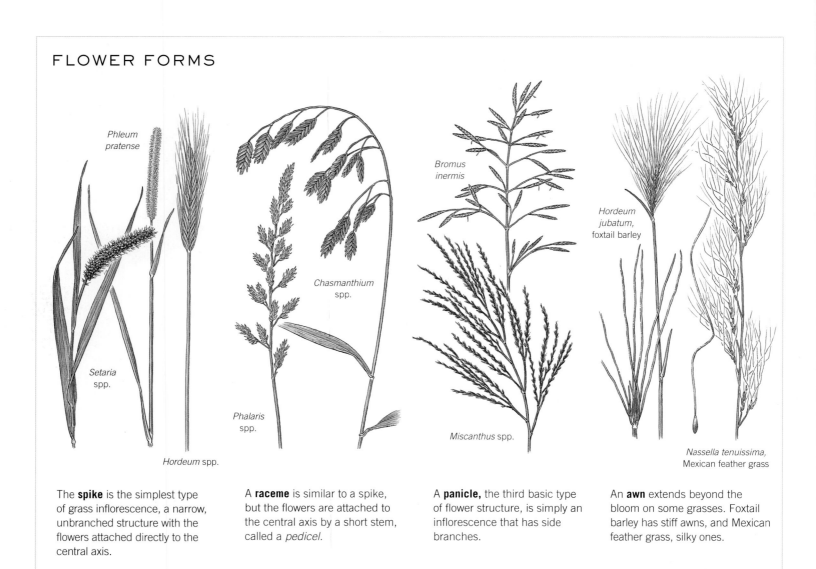

Phleum pratense

Setaria spp.

Hordeum spp.

Phalaris spp.

Chasmanthium spp.

Bromus inermis

Miscanthus spp.

Hordeum jubatum, foxtail barley

Nassella tenuissima, Mexican feather grass

The **spike** is the simplest type of grass inflorescence, a narrow, unbranched structure with the flowers attached directly to the central axis.

A **raceme** is similar to a spike, but the flowers are attached to the central axis by a short stem, called a *pedicel.*

A **panicle,** the third basic type of flower structure, is simply an inflorescence that has side branches.

An **awn** extends beyond the bloom on some grasses. Foxtail barley has stiff awns, and Mexican feather grass, silky ones.

Typical garden plants have showy flowers that do more than draw our attention: they also attract the various insects that they need for pollination. Grasses, however, depend on wind, rather than insects, to carry their pollen from flower to flower, so they don't need large, brightly colored blooms. Instead, they produce great numbers of tiny flowers, which are grouped into a cluster known as an *inflorescence*. Examples of different grass inflorescences are shown at the left, with the spike being the simplest. The individual flowers, called *florets*, are composed of the basic reproductive parts protected by tiny, scalelike structures called *bracts*.

Although grass flowers have a fairly limited color range, usually appearing in various shades of green, yellow, brown, pink, maroon, or silver, they make up for this as they subtly change and mature, turning tan, brown, gray, or gold. Some have a bristly or silky appearance, due to needlelike awns that extend out beyond the blooms.

Purple fountain grass (*Pennisetum setaceum* 'Rubrum'), with its spikelike raceme, has a brushy look, while Mexican feather grass *(Nassella tenuissima)* gets its silky appearance from long awns that extend from the spikelets.

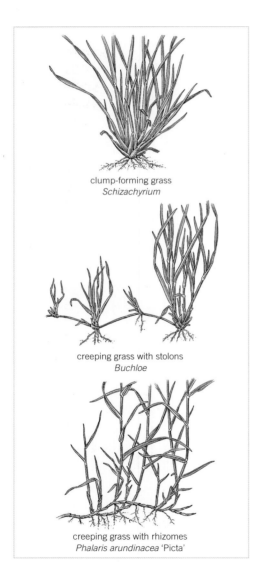

clump-forming grass
Schizachyrium

creeping grass with stolons
Buchloe

creeping grass with rhizomes
Phalaris arundinacea 'Picta'

CLUMPERS AND CREEPERS

Of all the various characteristics of grasses, perhaps the most important to understand when you are planning a garden is whether they are clump-forming or creeping. Clump-forming grasses grow in distinct tufts that expand slowly over time. Essentially, therefore, they stay where you put them. On the other hand, creeping grasses, also called *spreaders* or *runners*, produce vigorous horizontal stems that extend out over the ground or below it. Aboveground runners are called *stolons;* those below ground are called *rhizomes.* Some creepers form dense mats or carpets of foliage, whereas others pop up here and there, often surprisingly far from the original plant.

Clumpers are generally the grasses of choice for beds and borders, as you don't want bullies that will crowd out your other annuals and perennials, as creeping grasses may do. But creeping grasses have a place, too: they are ideal for holding the soil on a sloping site or for producing an easy-care ground cover for a less manicured area. Of course, it's possible to use creepers in beds and borders if you're willing to take control measures — either dividing them or digging out unwanted plants each year, or planting them in some sort of root barrier, such as a bottomless bucket sunk almost to its rim in the soil. Be aware, however, that these will need extra attention and work to keep them in check. A simpler way to enjoy creepers without the extra care is to grow them in aboveground pots and planters.

The softly brushed flower heads of clump-forming 'Hameln' fountain grass (*Pennisetum alopecuroides* 'Hameln') relate well to the similar texture of floss flower (*Ageratum houstonianum*).
(Chanticleer Garden, Wayne, Penn.)

SIZES AND SHAPES

There's an ornamental grass to suit any spot, from the tiniest balcony garden to the largest landscape. The plants range in height from just a few inches tall to a towering 20 feet or more, so it's important to investigate the mature height of any grass before you select it for your garden.

Ornamental grasses also grow in a variety of shapes, including tufted, upright, and mounded. Fescues, with their stiff, upright leaves growing from a central point, are good examples of a tufted grass. The more gracefully curved foliage of fountain grass is typical of a mounded grass, whereas the columnar form of switch grass exemplifies an upright grass.

Even more dramatic, a number of grasses have a combination of shapes. Their foliage might be mounded, for instance, but their flower stems are quite upright, as in feather reed grass *(Calamagrostis* x *acutiflora)*. Japanese silver grass *(Miscanthus sinensis),* on the other hand, has a combination of upright stems and arching foliage, which produces a fountainlike effect. The array of shapes and their changes through the season offer creative and adventuresome gardeners many opportunities for orchestrating exciting and unexpected effects.

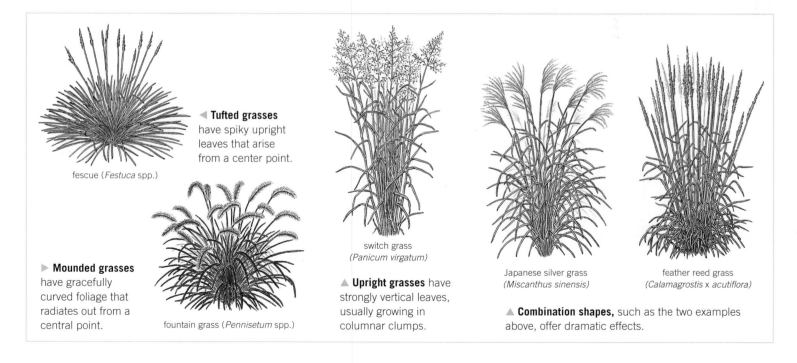

◀ **Tufted grasses** have spiky upright leaves that arise from a center point.

fescue (*Festuca* spp.)

▶ **Mounded grasses** have gracefully curved foliage that radiates out from a central point.

fountain grass (*Pennisetum* spp.)

switch grass (*Panicum virgatum*)

▲ **Upright grasses** have strongly vertical leaves, usually growing in columnar clumps.

Japanese silver grass (*Miscanthus sinensis*)

feather reed grass (*Calamagrostis* x *acutiflora*)

▲ **Combination shapes,** such as the two examples above, offer dramatic effects.

BEWARE, PROBLEM GRASSES

Grasses are among the most widespread plants in the wild because they are tough enough to compete with other plants for light, water, and nutrients. They're also quite successful at spreading themselves around, either through creeping roots or by producing copious amounts of seed. Though most ornamental grasses can coexist peacefully with other garden plants, some will require more work on your part. Knowing up front which grasses might be a problem will help you decide which to try and which to avoid.

Of course, it's possible to control just about any grass if you're willing to work at it. That might mean installing root barriers a

foot or more deep to contain the spread of creeping grasses. If self-sowing is the problem, you could mulch heavily each spring to smother the previous season's seeds before they sprout, or you could hoe or pull the unwanted seedlings by hand. Removing the spent flower heads before the seed ripens is another option, but by doing so you'd lose weeks or months of interest. If you want to get the most pleasure from your ornamental grasses with the least work, it makes sense to think carefully before you introduce a possible maintenance headache into your garden. Besides becoming garden weeds, some grasses can also escape into uncultivated areas, crowding out native vegetation and completely changing wildlife habitats.

Unfortunately, it's difficult to come up with a comprehensive list of "problem" grasses, because the same species can be a weed in one climate or site and an ideal garden plant in another. A grass that runs rampant in moist soil, for instance, will slow its spread dramatically if it reaches a dry site. And a species that readily self-sows in areas with a long frost-free season may produce few, if any, seedlings in cooler areas, where it won't have time to ripen its seeds. At the right is a list of grasses that are most likely to be troublesome. (For more information on the grasses that have weed potential in your area, ask the staff at your local nursery or botanical garden, or contact your local Cooperative Extension agent).

Cortaderia jubata (purple pampas grass): Can be a serious weed through self-sowing in mild climates.

Equisetum spp. (scouring rushes): Rhizomes spread rampantly in moist soil (shown at left).

Glyceria maxima 'Variegata' (variegated manna grass): Rhizomes spread quickly in moist soil.

Hordeum jubatum (foxtail barley): Self-sows readily.

Leymus arenarius (Lyme grass): Spreads quickly through rhizomes in loose soil.

Miscanthus sacchariflorus (silver banner grass): Spreads readily by rhizomes.

Miscanthus sinensis (Japanese silver grass): Early-flowering cultivars can self-sow and become weedy in warm climates.

Pennisetum spp. (fountain grasses): Tend to self-sow freely and can become weedy where hardy.

Phalaris arundinacea (gardener's garters): Variegated cultivars — those with more than one color in their leaves — can spread quickly by rhizomes.

Phyllostachys nigra (black bamboo): Spreads vigorously by rhizomes in the warmer parts of its hardiness range.

Pleioblastus viridistriatus (golden bamboo): Forms dense, outward-creeping colonies.

Typha spp. (cattails): Spread quickly by rhizomes in moist soil.

GROWTH CYCLES

Grasses have both annual and perennial forms. Annual grasses complete their life cycle — sprout from seed, grow, flower, set seed, and die — in one growing season. Perennial grasses, on the other hand, don't die after setting seed; instead, they come back year after year.

Among the perennial species, there are two basic types: cool-season and warm-season. Cool-season grasses start growing actively in late winter or early spring and usually flower in spring and early summer. Once temperatures rise above 75°F, they grow more slowly or go dormant altogether. Fescues (*Festuca* spp.) and golden wood millet (*Milium effusum* 'Aureum') are two cool-season grasses. Examples of warm-season grasses include evergreen miscanthus *(Miscanthus transmorrisonensis)*, pampas grass (*Cortaderia selloana*), and fountain grass (*Pennisetum* spp.).

Warm-season grasses, such as purple fountain grass (*Pennisetum setaceum*) (BELOW LEFT) and evergreen miscanthus (*Miscanthus transmorrisonensis)* (BELOW RIGHT), thrive in the heat, so they don't start growing until later in spring, and they tend to flower and set seed in late summer and fall.

THE LIGHT FANTASTIC

Typically, gardeners quantify light: How many hours of sun does a particular spot receive? How much light does this plant need to grow and thrive? But, importantly, light has an aesthetic component, a color and intensity that change through the day and season by season, and grasses are uniquely able to capture this quality.

Front lighting is the sort of effect we see when looking at a garden with the sun behind us. The light is harsh and does a good job displaying bright blooms, but it overpowers the subtle contrasts in form and texture that are so appealing in grasses. Grasses are at their best when illuminated from the side *(sidelighting)* or from the back *(backlighting)*.

Sidelighting creates dramatic contrasts between areas of brightness and shadow, delineating the distinctive shapes and textures of leaves, flowers, and seed heads. It's an excellent way to highlight grasses with delicate blooms that tend to get lost against a busy background of colorful leaves and flowers. Simply site the grasses against a dark background in an area where they will be lit by the sunrise or sunset, and they'll positively shimmer. As the quality of light changes, from the warm yellows of morning to the white light of midday to the soft rosy glow of early evening, lackluster flowers and seed heads are bathed in a rainbow of color.

Backlighting is another way you can create exquisite effects with ornamental grasses. When the sun is directly behind a grass, the plant is thrown into silhouette, revealing each amazing detail — a tiny hair, a feathery awn, a delicate flower, a seed — and the plant seems to glow from within. In some cases, the light may shine through the leaves, creating an effect much like that of light pouring through a stained-glass window.

It can be tricky to find the perfect way to take advantage of spectacular lighting effects in your garden. You might want

Backlit with sun, these grasses seem to glow from within. Clockwise from top left, giant feather grass *(Stipa gigantea)*, purple fountain grass (*Pennisetum setaceum* 'Rubrum'), and oriental fountain grass (*Pennisetum orientale*).

to grow your grasses in containers, then move them around until you find the most dramatic spot. Or, consider installing landscape lighting to create similar light effects in the evening.

TOP: Sunlit and tossed by gentle breezes, fine-textured Mexican feather grass *(Nassella tenuissima)* here almost appears to be a footlight for the roses in the background.

RIGHT: Fine-as-lace giant feather grass *(Stipa gigantea)* makes a glowing backdrop for the drooping, pink puffy flowers of ruby grass *(Rhynchelytrum nerviglume)*.

TEXTURAL TAPESTRIES

With color and beauty as our guides, many of us follow the color-at-all-costs approach to garden design. But with experience, we come to appreciate the contribution that texture makes in dynamic plant combinations. Ornamental grasses offer some of the most exciting and distinctive foliage textures.

Strongly linear patterns in mounds of showy 'Morning Light' miscanthus (*Miscanthus sinensis* 'Morning Light') surround softer-textured Russian sage *(Perovskia atriplicifolia)* and a cheerful sprinkling of yarrow (*Achillea* sp.).

Texture can refer to several different leaf traits: the shape of an individual leaf, the feel of the leaf surface, or the overall appearance of a plant in full leaf. As far as shape goes, leaves can be simple (made up of one leaf) or compound (with multiple leaflets attached to one leaf stem), and their edge can be entire (fairly uniform), lobed (with indenta-tions), or deeply divided. The surfaces usually fall into one of three main groups: smooth, hairy, or rough. And the look of a plant with its full comple-ment of leaves can be fine textured (with a lacy or feathery appearance), medium textured (most plants fall here), or coarse (think of broad-leaved hostas as an example).

Grasses vary widely in height, habit, and color, but they all share similar foliage textures. Their simple leaves tend to be long and narrow, with uniform edges. And while their surface can vary from smooth to rough to hairy, grass plants overall have an extremely fine-textured appearance: that's what makes them so valuable for creating striking combinations.

Many flowering border favorites have fairly nondescript foliage, but when you pair them with grasses, the leaves suddenly create an additional level of interest. Fine-textured masses of grass foliage make an outstanding backdrop for bold daisy-form flowers, for flat-topped or rounded flower clusters, and for dramatically shaped individual blooms, such as those of sea hollies (*Eryngium* spp.).

If you prefer foliage more than flowers, you'll enjoy situating fine-textured grasses next to big, bold leaves for an eye-catching contrast of forms. Grasses are also invaluable for softening "hardscape" features, such as walls, paved areas, steps, boulders, and other solid surfaces. Juxtaposing different textures creates a dramatic, exciting effect, while combining similar textures creates a restful feeling.

ABOVE: Often found in moist soils, sedges (*Carex* spp.) make appropriate companions for a container water garden. Here, graceful *Carex dolichostachya* 'Kaga Nishiki' (Gold Fountains) is nicely complemented by ferns and the coarser foliage of false holly (*Osmanthus heterophyllus* 'Ogon') by the tub. (Garden of Linda Cochran, Bainbridge Island, Wash.)

TOP RIGHT: Delicate and flowing, Mexican feather grass *(Nassella tenuissima)* makes a soothing break within a perennial border featuring bolder plants like the hybrid lilies in the foreground.

BOTTOM: A standout in any garden, the restio *Cannomois virgata* features sturdy green stems with red bracts, and drooping, hairlike foliage.

CHOOSING WISELY

As with any successful garden design, a garden filled with beautiful grasses starts with a thoughtful plan. Take time to deliberately choose the grasses best adapted to your climate, site, and needs. Study plant catalogs and visit nurseries and other gardens in your area before selecting the grasses for your own special spot.

The fescue *Festuca rupicola* partners with the yarrow *Achillea millefolium,* each thriving in sun and well-drained soil.

As with any plants you want to grow, success with grasses starts in choosing those that are best suited to your particular growing conditions. Begin by considering your climate. USDA hardiness zones provide a starting point by helping you determine whether a grass is likely to survive the winter in your area (for zone map, see page 128). But winter cold is just one factor. A cool-season grass, for instance, can certainly survive a mild southern winter, but it may not be able to tolerate the region's high summer heat. And while warmth-loving grasses usually don't thrive in colder climates, a site with excellent drainage and regular snow cover may provide ideal growing conditions where you'd least expect that grass to thrive. Other factors, such as humidity and coastal conditions, can also have a dramatic impact on how a certain grass grows for you. Throughout this book, you'll find a suggested hardiness range for many grasses: start there when making your selections, but feel free to experiment.

Next, evaluate the unique growing conditions — light, shade, soil quality, and moisture — that your property has to offer. The majority of grasses grow best in full sun, but some grasses can grow respectably well with less light, and some positively thrive with shade. Variegated grasses, for instance, often produce their best color in light shade. Most grasses grow well in "average" garden soil. Interestingly, overly fertile conditions can actually lead to floppy growth and poor flowering in grasses. Because they produce an extensive root system, many grasses are drought tolerant, but be aware that some species appreciate or demand a steady supply of moisture.

Along with their aesthetic qualities — foliage color, flowers, texture, height, and habit — there are two other things to consider when choosing grasses for your garden. First, can you tolerate spreading species, or are you looking for well-behaved clumpers? Both can have a place, but it's important to know which kind you're putting where, or you might inadvertently create a maintenance nightmare. And that leads to the second point: how much maintenance does a particular grass need? A species that requires frequent division, spreads rapidly, or produces many seedlings will need more attention than a long-lived, clump-forming, nonseeding grass.

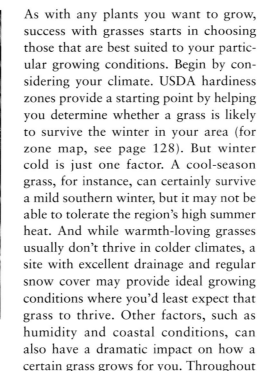

You may discover that finding the grasses you want to grow is far more difficult than actually growing them. Lack of demand may be one reason local garden centers carry only a limited selection. When compared to their flowering counterparts, potted grasses are simply less enticing to potential purchasers. However, market-savvy garden centers have started incorporating ornamental grasses into their display gardens to demonstrate how the featured grasses perform in a particular climate and to inspire potential customers to experiment in new ways with grass companions and combinations.

If you are not able to obtain what you need locally, many mail-order nurseries offer a wide selection of species and cultivars. Place your order in fall or winter (the earlier the better), and expect your shipment to arrive some time in spring. (There are a few exceptions: Some nurseries will ship cool-season grasses in fall, too. In addition, most wait until late spring or early summer to ship tender grasses to cooler climates.)

When you order by mail, don't expect to receive big, sturdy-looking plants. Hardy grasses are often shipped bare-root (with only packing material around

them), and the scrawny sprigs look decidedly unpromising. But have faith: plant them out or pot them up, water as needed to keep them from drying out, and in a few short weeks, they should settle in and begin thriving.

Golden Hakone grass (*Hakonechloa macra* 'Aureola') brightens a shady pathway in this Seattle garden.

How Do Your Grasses Grow?

Ornamental grasses aren't what you'd call no-maintenance plants, but they're definitely on the low-maintenance end of the fuss-and-muss spectrum. They'll thrive with the same good care you give your other garden plants, and they're normally not much bothered by pests or diseases.

Early spring is the ideal time to get warm-season grasses in the ground, so they can put down some roots and be ready to shoot upward as the temperatures start to rise. You can plant cool-season grasses any time, although early spring usually works best for them, too.

Don't go to a lot of bother with soil preparation — definitely hold off on the rich manures and fertilizers, as ornamental grasses don't enjoy an overly rich soil — but do loosen the soil as you would for any other plant. Be sure to rid the planting area of any weeds *before* you plant, particularly if you're plagued by pesky perennial grasses, such as quackgrass *(Agropyron repens)*. Trying to weed out unwanted grasses from your carefully chosen cultivars can be the gardener's ultimate nightmare.

Grasses should be spaced about as far apart as the mature plants will be tall. For smaller grasses, that equates to 12 to 30 inches apart; for taller ones, allow 4 to 5 feet between clumps. They will look a little sparse at first — especially if you're starting with small grass plants — but they will expand over time. If you want a fuller look faster, you could space the plants more closely, but then you'd need to dig up and divide the crowded clumps several years sooner than you would otherwise.

Plant grasses the way you would any other perennial. If you are planting a grass that's been growing in a container, water it well before removing it from the pot. Dig a planting hole that's large enough to hold the roots or root ball comfortably. It should be just deep enough that the crown of the

PLANTING GRASSES

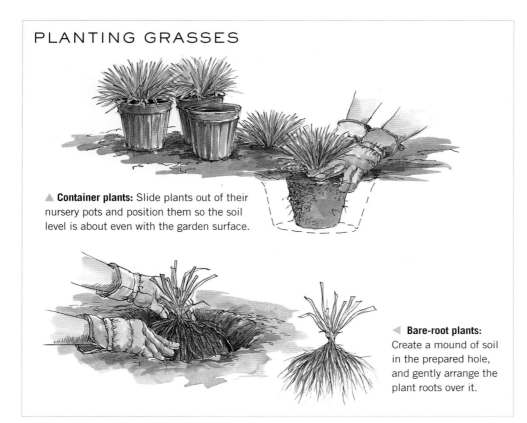

▲ **Container plants:** Slide plants out of their nursery pots and position them so the soil level is about even with the garden surface.

◀ **Bare-root plants:** Create a mound of soil in the prepared hole, and gently arrange the plant roots over it.

grass (where the leaves and stems come out of the roots) will be even with the soil surface, or slightly above. Slide the potted grasses out of their container and set them in the center of the hole. Or, if you're working with bare-root grasses, first make a mound of soil in the center of the hole, then set the crown on top and spread out the roots over the mound as evenly as you can.

Next, add more soil around the roots until the hole is about half full, then water generously. Let that water soak in for a few minutes, then finish filling the hole with soil, and water again. After planting, add an inch or two of mulch around the plant, being careful not to pile it right against the crown. It's important to allow room for air circulation, as excess moisture near the crown can promote rot.

FEEDING AND WATERING

Most grasses require minimal maintenance. You shouldn't fertilize heavily, because an excess of nitrogen can lead to lush, soft growth that tends to flop. Mulching with 1 to 2 inches of compost each year will help keep the soil and your plants in good shape. Water grasses regularly during their first year to help get a good root system established. Even grasses that are normally touted as drought-tolerant require a season or two to become fully established. If you've chosen grasses that are adapted to your climate, you shouldn't have to do much supplemental watering after the first year. If you decide to irrigate your grasses or if they're growing with other plants you'll be watering, use soaker

Gray-green deer grass *(Muhlenbergia rigens)* adapts to both moist and dry conditions but grows nearly twice as tall with abundant water.

hoses to direct water to the roots while keeping the leaves dry, thereby minimizing disease problems.

Be aware that watering can have a dramatic effect on the height and the sturdiness of certain grasses. Deer grass *(Muhlenbergia rigens)*, for instance, grows about 2 feet tall in dry conditions, but when it gets plenty of moisture that height can double. Keeping the soil a little on the dry side can help keep often-floppy grasses, like some miscanthus *(Miscanthus* spp.), from getting too lush and sprawling.

THE CHOICE IS YOURS

Deadheading grasses can be a matter of aesthetics or a matter of sanity. In the former case, you might choose to snip off the flowers in favor of the prettier foliage or just leave them alone if you don't have time. With some grasses, though, sparing the clippers can spoil your garden — or at the very least give you more weeding to do. Of course, removing the flowers before they set seed will eliminate weeks or months of enjoyment. But, on the other hand, if you remove the unwanted seedlings, it could save you years of laborious weeding. Prime candidates for deadheading include the following:

Bottlebrush grass *(Hystrix patula)*
Broomsedges *(Andropogon* spp.)
Fountain grasses *(Pennisetum* spp.)
Indian grass *(Sorghastrum nutans)*
Japanese silver grass *(Miscanthus sinensis)*
Korean feather reed grass *(Calamagrostis brachytricha)*
Melic grasses *(Melica* spp.)
Perennial quaking grass *(Briza media)*
Switch grass *(Panicum virgatum)*
Tufted hair grass *(Deschampsia cespitosa)*
Wild oats *(Chasmanthium latifolium)*

CUTTING BACK

The principal task with grasses is cutting them back to remove old foliage. Many gardeners like to cut down and clean up their gardens in fall, and that's fine for grasses that usually don't last well into winter, including giant reed *(Arundo donax)*, hair grass *(Deschampsia* spp.), Lyme grass *(Leymus arenarius)*, blood grass *(Imperata cylindrica* var. *koenigii* 'Red Baron'), and ravenna grass *(Saccharum ravennae)*. Cutting back all dried grasses makes good sense — and even is required by law in some locales — if you live where wildfires are a frequent problem.

Having said that, there are some compelling reasons to let warm-season grasses stand for the winter, if you can. For instance, leaving the foliage intact can help protect the plant's crown from cold and moisture, minimizing the chance of winter rot. In addition, you'll be able to enjoy the beauty of the seed heads and the foliage, and wild birds will appreciate the seeds and shelter. By the time the top growth starts to lose its appeal — in late winter or early spring — you can cut it down to 4 to 6 inches above the ground to let the fresh new growth emerge.

Cool-season grasses go dormant during hot weather, so they'll need a little atten-

tion in early to midsummer to keep their good looks. For some, such as blue oat grass *(Helictotrichon sempervirens)*, grooming is simply a matter of raking or plucking out the dead foliage. On others, you may want to cut back the top growth by about half to get a flush of fresh new foliage for fall. This works well with Lyme grass, hair grasses, ribbon grass *(Phalaris arundinacea* 'Picta'), and perennial quaking grass *(Briza media)*.

For cutting back a small grass, hand-held pruning or grass shears work just fine. Larger grasses need more powerful tools, such as electric hedge shears or even a power trimmer with a blade attachment. The leaves of some grasses

Use twine to bundle the grasses before cutting them close to the ground.

have surprisingly sharp edges, so wear gloves, eye protection, long sleeves, and long pants when cutting down your plants. Before cutting, make sure there are no forgotten metal stakes in the ground that might be hidden by the foliage. Tying up the top growth with twine before cutting can make cleanup a snap: you'll have one neatly tied bundle to pick up, instead of having to rake up dozens of stalks that are scattered throughout the garden.

STAKING

Unless you're one of the few gardeners who actually *enjoy* staking, it makes sense to keep this task to a minimum. Consider using more compact cultivars of normally tall grasses, such as miscanthus, and use fertilizers and supplemental watering sparingly. By dividing large clumps you can help minimize flopping due to overcrowding, but if you've ever tried to lift a large, established clump, you may decide that staking is easier. One trick you might try is cutting your tall grasses back to about 6 inches above the ground in early to midsummer. The resulting regrowth will be much shorter, and your plants will likely flower a bit later than usual. This approach can be a real stake-saver with tall grasses such as

miscanthus, prairie cord grass *(Spartina pectinata)*, and ravenna grass *(Saccharum ravennae)*.

If you do decide to stake your plants, metal pipes, commercial metal hoops, or sturdy wood or rebar stakes and twine can all serve the purpose. Just make sure to get the supports in the ground early, so the stalks can grow up through and cover them.

Prairie cord grass *(Spartina pectinata)* and other large grasses can help support each other when planted in masses, but you still may need to stake or trim clumps close to walkways to keep them from blocking the path.

DIVIDING GRASSES

◀ To divide creeping grasses, simply dig them up, gently pull them apart, and replant.

▶ Use a sharp spade to cut a wedge out of the side of a large clump of grass and replant the smaller piece. Fill in around the old plant with additional soil.

DIVIDING

As mentioned previously, division can be useful for rejuvenating sprawling, overgrown grasses, but there are also other reasons to divide. Some densely tufting grasses, such as fescues (*Festuca* spp.), tend to be short-lived unless you divide and replant them every two or three years. You may also notice that dense clump-formers develop a hole in the center as the inner growth gets shaded out; division is one solution here. (An easier option on large grasses is to hollow out the hole with a spade or post-hole digger, refill it with fresh soil, and set a small plant of the same grass right in the center to fill the spot.) Lifting, dividing, and replanting just a few pieces is one way to help control grasses with spreading tendencies. And last, division is an efficient way to propagate your grasses, to expand your own plantings, and to share them with your gardening friends.

Ideally, divide any grass when it is getting ready to start active growth. For cool-season grasses, that generally means early spring. (Early fall is another option, but if you live where the soil tends to freeze and thaw often, clumps divided in fall may get heaved out of the soil.) Wait until mid- to late spring, or even early summer, to divide warm-season grasses.

Division is a simple task with creeping grasses: just dig them up, pull them apart, and replant. To divide small clumps, lift them with a trowel or spading fork, and pull or cut them into several sections. You'll need a strong spade and a strong back to lift the biggest grasses and an ax or chain saw to divide them. For an easier method, simply cut wedges out of the edges of the clumps, leaving the main part of the plant in place and filling in the holes with fresh soil. Larger divisions will reestablish most quickly, but you can make several smaller pieces if you wish; just be sure each new piece has some roots.

Preventing Problems

One of the most appealing characteristics of ornamental grasses is their relative resistance to pests and diseases. That's not to say they are immune, of course. In the disease department, *rust,* a fungal disease that produces powdery orange patches on leaves and stems, is a common problem. While it normally isn't serious enough to kill an established grass plant, rust can spread quickly in humid conditions, particularly when days are warm and nights are cool. To prevent problems, avoid crowding your grasses too closely together, and use soaker hoses to minimize moisture around the leaves. If you spot just a few rusty-looking, yellow, or browned leaves, pinch them off immediately; if the whole plant is affected, cut off all the foliage a few inches above the soil.

As far as pests are concerned, you may see aphids feeding on lush new growth, but the plants generally grow so quickly that damage is minimized with no intervention from you. Mealybugs are slowly becoming a serious pest on miscanthus. These small, cottony white insects cluster and feed where the leaves join the stems, causing stunted, distorted growth. It's extremely difficult to control these pests, so inspect any miscanthus plants carefully before you buy them. If you already have plants with this problem, dig them up and destroy them; don't compost them.

Rabbits, deer, and other animal pests may nibble on your plants, but they seldom do serious damage, especially on sharp-leaved grasses such as miscanthus and prairie cord grass. In the western United States, gophers can be a major problem, devouring even long-established grasses with little warning. Where these critters are active, the best control is prevention. Try digging extra-large planting holes (about twice as big as usual) and lining the walls of the hole with wire mesh before replacing some of the soil and then planting as usual. You may also be able to find ready-made metal baskets at your local garden center that provide the same protection for the roots of your plants.

Small, white, and cottonlike, mealybugs cluster where leaves join stems.

COLOR PALETTES

ABOVE: Backed by violet-blue *Caryopteris,* the bronze foliage of New Zealand hair sedge *(Carex comans)* picks up the color of the distinctive cones of the purple coneflower *(Echinacea purpurea).*

OPPOSITE: Silver-tan flower heads of *Miscanthus sinensis* (left) and orange *Calamagrostis* x *acutiflora* 'Karl Foerster' (background) are stunning foils for a sea of lavender, punctuated by deep rose *Lavatera* blossoms.

Ornamental grasses come in an astounding array of hues and shades, from bright red and gold to copper, bronze, steel blue, and silver. The colors of some change to punctuate the seasons, creating variety that gardeners anticipate with delight; others offer consistent foliage color. A single colorful grass, such as the rich reddish purple fountain grass (*Pennisetum setaceum* 'Rubrum'), can add welcome drama to a simple container planting from spring to frost; in masses, it makes a striking long-season landscape accent.

Grasses that change color throughout the year present a challenge, albeit an enjoyable one. With some grasses, spring color is most vivid, as with the sunny yellow foliage of golden wood millet (*Milium effusum* 'Aureum') or the bright white stripes of variegated bulbous oat grass (*Arrhenatherum elatius* ssp. *bulbosum* 'Variegatum'). These early birds are carefree companions for other spring beauties, including tulips, forget-me-nots *(Myosotis sylvatica),* and bleeding hearts (*Dicentra* spp.). Other ornamental grasses are at their most vivid in late summer and fall. The plain green early foliage bides its time while spring and early summer flowers take the stage, then gradually steps to the fore in a colorful show as summer progresses. Fall invites still more varied hues, with the changing shades of warm-season grasses fading to subdued rusts, bronzes, and golds after frost.

Ornamental grasses offer a vibrant color palette for the garden. May the images that follow inspire you to explore color in new, perhaps unexpected ways.

GLOWING GOLDS AND BRONZES

If you enjoy growing and using plants with colorful foliage, you'll find many golden and bronze grasses to add to your plant palette. Many of these grasses are striking enough to stand alone, but showcasing them with carefully chosen annual and perennial companions accentuates their true beauty.

Golden Hakone grass (*Hakonechloa macra* 'Aureola') pairs with a variegated form of the shrub elaeagnus *(Elaeagnus pungens maculata),* getting a jolt of contrast from the lacey, purple foliage of Japanese maple *(Acer palmatum).*

(Garden of Linda Cochran, Bainbridge Island, Wash.)

Gold- and yellow-leaved grasses are particularly well suited for making exciting color combinations. Create a simple but handsome contrast by pairing a bright yellow or gold grass with a dark-green-leaved companion; for example, to add drama to a shady site, try golden wood millet (*Milium effusum* 'Aureum') against the daphnelike foliage of Robb's wood spurge *(Euphorbia robbiae).* For a cool-color combination and fabulous textural contrast, pair a golden grass with the bold foliage of a blue-leaved or blue-and-gold variegated hosta, such as 'Halcyon' or 'Aurora Borealis'. If you want a more daring display, combine golden grasses with plants having moody purple, maroon, or black foliage. Picture, if you will, golden greater wood rush (*Luzula sylvatica* 'Aurea') spiking up through the lacy, near-black leaves of 'Ravenswing' anthriscus (*Anthriscus sylvestris* 'Ravenswing'), or the glowing foliage of Bowles' golden sedge (*Carex elata* 'Aurea') spilling over the broad foliage of 'Chocolate Ruffles' heuchera (*Heuchera* hybrid 'Chocolate Ruffles'). With just two foliage plants, you can create a memorable, can't-miss accent that lasts from spring to frost.

That's not to say that golden grasses don't look great with flowers, because they definitely do. In fact, apart from pale and brassy yellows, it's difficult to think of a flower color that these grasses wouldn't pair well with. Golden grass foliage makes an especially elegant accent for chartreuse blooms, such as those of lady's mantle *(Alchemilla mollis),* euphorbia *(Euphorbia* spp.), and green-flowering tobacco *(Nicotiana langsdorfii)*. Another combination that I find especially appealing is blue (or purple) and gold, so I generally like to plant gold-leaved grasses with bellflower *(Campanula* spp.), balloon flower *(Platycodon grandiflorus)*, forget-me-nots *(Myosotis sylvatica)*, and Siberian iris *(Iris sibirica)*. If your tastes differ, by all means try these grasses with the flower colors you prefer; you'll be glad you did.

Gold- and yellow-leaved grasses generally do fine in full sun in cooler climates. In hot-summer areas, though, strong afternoon sun can cause the foliage to bleach out or turn brassy or brown; in these areas, a site with light shade all day or with morning sun and afternoon shade is desirable. Striving to keep the soil evenly moist can also help to prevent golden grasses from scorching.

The individual species of bronze-leaved sedges vary somewhat in their needs, but generally they prefer soil that is evenly moist and has excellent drainage — a combination that can be somewhat challenging to provide. It's worth experimenting with the half dozen or so bronze-leaved forms and species available to see which perform best under your particular conditions.

A STUDY IN SUBTLETY

At first thought, the idea of intentionally planting a brown-leaved grass may seem like a horrible horticultural joke. After all, why would anyone bother planting something that already looks dead? Once you get past the initial shock, though, you may find that these bronze-leaved grasses become seasonal favorites.

To begin, let's set the record straight: what we're calling bronze-leaved grasses aren't really grasses at all. Instead, they're a group of sedges *(Carex* spp.) that hail from New Zealand. By any name, they're fascinating plants that can add interest to beds, borders, pots, and planters. Orange-brown-toned sedges are particularly effective as a transition between brightly colored blooms. Coppery-bronze sedges, such as the New Zealand hair sedge *(Carex comans)* pictured below, complement softer flower colors, including buttery yellow, rosy pink, salmon orange, and lilac purple. And they're simply stunning when paired with silvery foliage, such as that of lamb's ears *(Stachys byzantina)* and 'Powis Castle' artemisia *(Artemisia* 'Powis Castle').

Carex comans 'Bronze'

Liriope muscari 'PeeDee Ingot'

Hakonechloa macra 'Aureola'

GOLDS AND BRONZES

Carex comans 'Bronze'
'Bronze' New Zealand hair sedge
Dense, swirling, 1-foot-tall clumps of hairlike, copper-brown foliage. Many other brown-leaved sedges are also available, including *C. buchananii, C. flagellifera, C. petrei,* and *C. testacea.* Full sun (light shade in hot climates); average to moist, well-drained soil. *Zones 7 to 9*

Carex elata 'Aurea'
Bowles' golden sedge
Two-foot-tall clumps of slender leaves that are mostly yellow with faint green vertical stripes. Full sun (for best color) to light shade; evenly moist soil. *Zones 5 to 9*

Deschampsia flexuosa 'Aurea'
Golden crinkled hair grass
Dense, 1-foot-tall clumps of shiny, fine-textured, yellow-green foliage; airy panicles of glossy spikelets atop 2-foot-tall stems in midsummer. Light shade; moist, humus-rich, well-drained soil. *Zones 4 to 9*

Hakonechloa macra 'Aureola'
Golden Hakone grass
Slowly expanding, 1- to 2-foot-tall mounds of arching, glossy green leaves with broad yellow stripes; may have pink tints in cool conditions. Full sun if cool and moist, otherwise best in light to partial shade; evenly moist, humus-rich, well-drained soil. *Zones 5 to 9*

Liriope muscari 'PeeDee Ingot'
'PeeDee Ingot' blue lilyturf
Slow-spreading clumps of slender, arching, bright yellow leaves usually about 8 inches tall; deep purple flower spikes in fall. Partial to full shade; humus-rich, well-drained soil. *Zones 6 to 9*

Pleioblastus viridistriatus
Golden bamboo
Also known as *Arundinaria viridistriata* or *Pleioblastus auricomus*; dense, 2- to 3-foot-tall, fast-spreading colonies of slender, upright stems clad in bright green leaves with irregular, bright yellow stripes; rarely flowers. Full sun to partial shade; average soil, drought tolerant when established. *Zones 5 to 10*

A Study in Gold

Golden foliage glows warmly even in light shade in this simple but stunning combination at Heronswood Nursery, Kingston, Washington — a brightener in any garden. The golds are thrown into even greater relief by the startlingly vivid flower spikes of catmint *(Nepeta sibirica)*.

A delightful display of color and texture in early summer, this garden nook remains beautiful long after the flowers have faded because of the well-chosen grasses. The show begins in early spring, when the bright yellow blades of golden wood millet *(Milium effusum* 'Aureum') appear. By early summer, its airy seed heads offer a striking counterpoint to the dense globes of the ornamental onion *(Allium* sp.) blooms. The millet tends to self-sow, and it can get a bit tired looking by the time the seeds form, so you might want to cut it back rather severely to prevent unwanted seedlings and to encourage a flush of fresh new foliage. While its companions change with the seasons, the swirling foliage of 'Bronze' New Zealand hair sedge *(Carex comans* 'Bronze') offers steadfast, ground-level grace throughout the season.

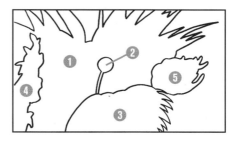

1. *Milium effusum* 'Aureum', golden wood millet
2. *Allium* sp., ornamental onion
3. *Carex comans* 'Bronze', 'Bronze' New Zealand hair sedge
4. *Papaver* sp., poppy
5. *Nepeta sibirica*, catmint

COOL BLUES AND QUIET GRAYS

No matter what your color preferences, blue grasses, in all their many shades and gradations, from bright blue to nearly gray, can serve several purposes in a garden scheme. Some blues blend beautifully with soft colors, while others make outstanding accents for more intensely colored plants.

Powder-blue grasses are especially lovely in early summer combinations with pastel flowers and foliage: consider using 'Elijah Blue' fescue (*Festuca glauca* 'Elijah Blue') with soft yellow foxgloves *(Digitalis lutea)* and rosy cheddar pinks *(Dianthus gratianopolitanus)*. Carry that theme through the summer with blue oat grass *(Helictotrichon sempervirens)*, buttery 'Moonbeam' coreopsis (*Coreopsis verticillata* 'Moonbeam'), and pink 'Shortwood' phlox (*Phlox* 'Shortwood'), then finish up in fall with 'Cloud Nine' switch grass (*Panicum virgatum* 'Cloud Nine'), light yellow 'Lemon Queen' sunflower (*Helianthus* 'Lemon Queen'), and pink 'September Charm' anemone (*Anemone hupehensis* 'September Charm').

For a particularly elegant effect, try pairing blue-leaved grasses with blue flowers. Let wispy love-in-a-mist (*Nigella damascena*) weave up through spiky blue oat grass, or use Magellan wheatgrass (*Elymus magellanicus*) as an exquisite accompaniment for the steel-blue blooms of sea holly (*Eryngium* spp.) and globe thistle (*Echinops* spp.). White flowers —

including 'Gourmet Popcorn' miniature rose, white rose campion (*Lychnis coronaria* 'Alba'), and white tulips, to name just a few — are also charming companions for the blue grasses.

Do you long for "edgier" plant combinations? Consider taking a trip across the color wheel and contrast blue grasses with brightly colored blooms in the red-orange-yellow range. Blue-leaved switch grasses, such as 'Heavy Metal' and 'Dallas Blues', for instance, provide an icy-cool backdrop for the plum-colored new foliage, red buds, and cherry red blooms of the floribunda rose aptly named 'Knock Out'. If you're truly adventurous with color, you might experiment by pairing a blue-gray grass with clear orange classic zinnia (*Zinnia angustifolia*). Or take a page out of Mother Nature's gardening notebook, and pair the orange-yellow blooms of black-eyed Susan (*Rudbeckia* spp.) with the blue-green leaves of 'Sioux Blue' Indian grass (*Sorghastrum nutans* 'Sioux Blue').

Plants with intensely colored foliage also make fabulous accompaniments

Blue oat grass *(Helictotrichon sempervirens)* unifies a cheerful grouping of *Heliopsis helianthoides* 'Summer Sun', *Asclepias,* and *Achillea.*

for blue-leaved grasses. For contrasting colors but similar texture, try black mondo grass (*Ophiopogon planiscapus* 'Nigrescens') in front of a medium-height blue grass, such as 'The Blues' little bluestem (*Schizachyrium scoparium* 'The Blues'). Or contrast both color and texture by pairing a cool, blue-leaved grass with the broad foliage of a dark-leaved heuchera (perhaps 'Purple Petticoats') or a warm, golden hosta, such as 'Sun Power'.

The grasses in this color group vary widely in their growing needs, so it's worthwhile to do some research and thoroughly investigate all those you can find before deciding which will work best for you. Some are quite drought tolerant; others prefer more moisture. Some produce their most intense color in spring and early summer; others are at their peak in late summer and fall. Blue and gray grasses as a group seem to thrive in full sun. Many can tolerate light shade, but, like many other ornamental grasses, the less sun they get, the less intense their color.

Cool complementary colors are a fitting backdrop for the popular blue fescue *Festuca idahoensis* 'Siskiyou Blue', here paired with a deep purple iris.

Festuca glauca

Helictotrichon sempervirens

Juncus patens 'Occidental Blue'

BLUES AND GRAYS

Festuca glauca
Blue fescue
Tight 6- to 10-inch tufts of fine-textured, blue-green or gray-green foliage. Blue-green flower panicles on 12- to 18-inch stems in early summer; shear plants lightly after flowering to remove blooms and shape plants. Full sun (takes light shade in hot climates); average, well-drained soil. *Zones 4 to 8*

Helictotrichon sempervirens
Blue oat grass
Dense, 12- to 18-inch clumps of narrow, blue-gray leaves that are evergreen in mild climates and semi-evergreen in cooler areas. Early-summer flowers are greenish to tan, oatlike panicles held well above the foliage on 3- to 4-foot stems. Full sun; fertile, well-drained soil. *Zones 4 to 9*

Juncus patens
California gray rush
Spiky, 18- to 30-inch, evergreen clumps of slender, upright, gray-green stems. 'Occidental Blue' has very blue foliage. Sun to light shade; moist to wet, fertile soil. *Zones 7 to 9*

Koeleria glauca
Blue hair grass
Dense, 6- to 12-inch, evergreen mounds of blue-green foliage. Full sun; average to poor, well-drained soil. *Zones 6 to 9*

Panicum virgatum 'Cloud Nine'
'Cloud Nine' switch grass
Four- to 6-foot, upright clumps of grayish green leaves that turn golden yellow in fall, then tan in winter. Full sun to light shade; adaptable, tolerates dry to wet soil. *Zones 4 to 9*

Schizachyrium scoparium 'The Blues'
'The Blues' little bluestem
Also known as *Andropogon scoparius* 'The Blues'; forms 3- to 4-foot-tall clumps of mostly upright, silvery blue stems and leaves that turn orange to reddish brown in fall. Full sun (tolerates light shade); good drought tolerance but best in evenly moist, well-drained soil. *Zones 3 to 9*

Sorghastrum nutans 'Sioux Blue'
'Sioux Blue' Indian grass
Upright, 3- to 4-foot-tall clumps of distinctly blue-green leaves that turn yellow in fall, then tan in winter. Full sun (tolerates light shade); most vigorous in moist soil but drought-tolerant when established. *Zones 4 to 9*

GROWING THE BLUES

Blue-leaved grasses are wonderfully versatile. Pair them with pinks and yellows to bring pastel charms to any season, or use them with bright reds and yellows for a dynamic palette of primary colors.

This display at Elisabeth C. Miller Botanical Garden in Seattle celebrates subtlety by pairing bright 'Siskiyou Blue' Idaho fescue (*Festuca idahoensis* 'Siskiyou Blue') with the muted blue-green foliage of shrubby cinquefoil (*Potentilla fruticosa*) and the rosy purple flowers of big betony (*Stachys macrantha* 'Superba'). This combination offers appealing textural contrasts early in the season, with the spiky blue fescue tucked behind the lacy leaves of cinquefoil and backed by a solid mass of pinkish purple blooms. As the fescue blossoms, the effect softens, the deep purple betony taking on a misty, ethereal quality.

As summer wears on, the fescue flower and seed heads gradually age to tan. When they do, you might want to shear the plants lightly, to trim off the unsightly tan and to shape the plants. Divide fescues every two to three years to help ensure continued growth and vibrant seasonal color.

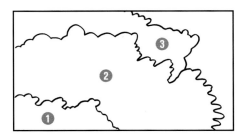

1. *Potentilla fruticosa*, shrubby cinquefoil

2. *Festuca idahoensis* 'Siskiyou Blue', 'Siskiyou Blue' Idaho fescue

3. *Stachys macrantha* 'Superba', big betony

DARKLY DRAMATIC

Of all the colors of grass foliage, the darker hues are among the most remarkable. Ranging from ruby red to nearly pure black, these amazing grasses are invaluable tools for creating unforgettable combinations in every part of your garden, whether they complement other plants or are themselves the stars of the show.

Dark-leaved grasses are outstanding in mid- to late-summer beds and borders, when hot-colored annuals and perennials are really putting on a show. Pure orange, scorching scarlet, glowing crimson, and school-bus yellow — the red-, maroon-, and black-leaved grasses work well with them all. Unlike green grasses, which can intensify the contrast between brightly colored flowers, dark-leaved selections offer a tranquil backdrop, a place for your eye to rest before exploring the next brilliant bloom. Scattered throughout a hot-colored border, dark-leaved grasses can unify the whole planting, no matter how eclectic your other color choices.

Dark-leaved grasses are also elegant in more subdued partnerships. Maroon-leaved fountain grasses (*Pennisetum* spp.) look lovely with a wide range of pink flowers, as well as peach, coral, rust, and other sunset shades. They also echo the dark centers of black-eyed Susan (*Rudbeckia* spp.) quite beautifully.

As far as foliage partners go, red-, maroon-, and black-leaved grasses pair well with many different colors. They're especially spectacular against silvery foliage, such as lamb's ears *(Stachys byzantina)* and artemisia (*Artemisia* spp.). Plants with chartreuse foliage — including golden feverfew (*Tanacetum parthenium*

'Aureum') and golden creeping Jenny (*Lysimachia nummularia* 'Aurea'), to name a few — also make perfect companions for dark-leaved grasses.

It's difficult to generalize about the growing needs of the grasses in this color range, particularly because many of them aren't even true grasses — they just have grasslike leaves. One trait that most share is their preference for plenty of sun. Too much shade tends to fade red and purple hues, bringing out more green and muddying the overall effect. Equally important, grown in a dark spot, these grasses cannot truly be appreciated.

When you're placing dark-leaved grasses in your garden, try to situate them against a lighter background, or pair them with bright blooms or contrasting foliage; otherwise, they may get lost among other dark colors and be overlooked. It's generally best to use these dark-leaved beauties somewhat sparingly — a few dark grasses are dramatic; too many can create a "black hole" in your border.

Moody and effective, richly dark purple fountain grass (*Pennisetum setaceum* 'Rubrum'), lavender, and *Phormium* 'Baby Bronze' unite a massing of *Miscanthus* in the background with Mexican feather grass *(Nassella tenuissima)* in front.

Imperata cylindrica var. *koenigii* 'Red Baron'

Pennisetum setaceum 'Rubrum'

Uncinia rubra

DARK-LEAVED GRASSES

Imperata cylindrica var. *koenigii* 'Red Baron'
Japanese blood grass
Slow-spreading clumps of 12- to 18-inch-tall upright leaves that emerge green with red tips in spring, turning totally red by late summer and fall and coppery in winter. Full sun (for best color) to light shade; evenly moist, well-drained soil. *Zones 6 to 9*

Pennisetum 'Burgundy Giant'
'Burgundy Giant' fountain grass
Four- to 5-foot-tall clumps of upright stems with broad, arching, deep reddish purple leaves. Full sun; evenly moist but well-drained soil. *Zones 9 to 10 (grow as an annual elsewhere)*

Pennisetum setaceum 'Rubrum'
Purple fountain grass
Also known as *Pennisetum setaceum* 'Atrosanguineum', 'Cupreum', or 'Purpureum'; develops 3- to 4-foot-tall clumps of arching, glossy, purplish red leaves. Full sun; evenly moist but well-drained, fertile soil. *Zones 9 to 10 (grow as an annual elsewhere)*

Saccharum officinarum 'Pele's Smoke'
'Pele's Smoke' sugarcane
Dark reddish purple, arching leaves on stout, upright, near-black stems with cream-colored nodes; height is 10 to 15 feet where the plants are hardy, usually 6 to 8 feet elsewhere. Full sun; adaptable but best in evenly moist, well-drained soil. *Zone 10 (grow as an annual elsewhere)*

Uncinia rubra
Red hook sedge
Also known as *Uncinia uncinata* 'Rubra'; dense, 1-foot-tall clumps of glossy, deep bronze-red, evergreen leaves; dark brown flowers in mid- to late summer. Full sun; average to evenly moist soil. *Zones 8 to 10*

RICHLY RED

Few garden plants offer red foliage, so those that do make invaluable additions to your garden palette. A number of grasses, sedges, and their relatives produce leaves in vivid, varied hues, providing rich textural and color contrasts.

Definitely not for the faint of heart, this red New Zealand flax (*Phormium* 'Maori Maiden') creates an arresting accent wherever you site it. Here, at Strybing Arboretum, San Francisco, it is artfully surrounded by appealing but less dramatic companion grasses, such as Sun Stripe pampas grass (*Cortaderia selloana* 'Monvin'), as well as small bright blooms (poppies and oxalis) that echo the garden's focal point. North of Zone 8, bring the flax indoors for the winter, or use instead a hardy red-leaved grass, like Japanese blood grass (*Imperata cylindrica* var. *koenigii* 'Red Baron').

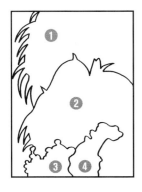

1. *Cortaderia selloana* 'Monvin', Sun Stripe pampas grass

2. *Phormium* 'Maori Maiden', 'Maori Maiden' New Zealand flax

3. *Papaver* sp., poppy

4. *Oxalis spiralis*, oxalis

Variety, the Spice of Life

Variegated grasses are an appropriate option when you want to spark your garden with color. Not only do these multicolored standouts contrast handsomely with all-green grasses, but they also make elegant companions for flowers. Especially effective designs use flower colors that pick up the yellow or white markings of the grasses.

DOS AND DON'TS

• Do keep a wary eye for all-green shoots appearing in your variegated grasses, and remove them as soon as you see them. Often far more vigorous than their multicolored cousins, these reverted shoots can quickly take over the clump. You can use the reduced vigor of variegates to your advantage, however. Variegated forms of creeping grasses generally spread more slowly than the all-green versions, so they can be somewhat easier to control where space is limited.

• Don't plant variegates next to one another unless they are distinctly different in color, texture, or form. Otherwise, they will blend together visually, and you'll lose the drama that the individual plants can provide if you separate them with different foliage or flower colors.

Variegations usually appear as long stripes running the length of the leaf (often along the edges, or down the center), although a few have short bands of color that span the leaf's width.

Some variegated grasses literally "change their stripes" during the growing season. For example, zebra grass (*Miscanthus sinensis* 'Zebrinus') and 'Oehme' palm sedge (*Carex muskingumensis* 'Oehme') tend to be all green when they first emerge, developing their variegation in late spring to early summer. Variegated giant reed (*Arundo donax* 'Variegata') has bright white stripes in spring, but by midsummer, the stripes are more cream colored. Cool spring and fall temperatures can cause the leaves of Feesey's gardener's garters (*Phalaris arundinacea* 'Feesey') to take on pinkish hues.

Dramatic as landscape features, these vibrant selections also make marvelous additions to mixed plantings of perennials, annuals, bulbs, and shrubs. Set against darker colors, bright white- or yellow-striped grasses create eye-catching accents. A variegated grass can easily enhance a particular color theme, such as an all-white garden.

Variegated grasses offer a logical focus for monochromatic combinations. Those cultivars with yellow markings make excellent complements for yellow flowers. The pale yellow bands of 'Little Dot' miscanthus (*Miscanthus sinensis* 'Little Dot', also known as 'Puenktchen'), for example, deftly echo the soft yellow

Skinner's gold brome *(Bromus inermis* 'Skinner's Gold') has elegant gold leaves brushed with both dark and light green.
(Elizabeth C. Miller Botanical Garden, Seattle)

blooms of 'Moonbeam' coreopsis (*Coreopsis verticillata* 'Moonbeam'). Similarly, white-striped grasses make charming partners for white flowers. Use *Miscanthus sinensis* 'Rigoletto' with Shasta daisies or a white *Cleome,* for example, or feature white-painted garden accents, like picket fences, trellises, and arbors.

Most variegated grasses perform best in light, all-day shade or in morning sun and partial afternoon shade. Too much sun can scorch white stripes, turning them brown, especially when the soil is rather dry. Heavy shade, on the other hand, can cause variegated grasses to turn nearly or completely green. If you're not sure how a variegate will perform in a site you have in mind, consider growing it there in a pot for a season as a test. If it holds its color well, go ahead and plant it; otherwise, move the pot to a different spot and observe it for another season.

Even before it bears its characteristic plumes, *Cortaderia selloana* 'Silver Comet' brings grace and light to this tropical-looking combination that includes (clockwise from top left) *Hibiscus, Canna, and Eupatorium,* and, in the left corner, *Colocasia.*

Acorus gramineus 'Ogon'

Miscanthus sinensis 'Strictus'

Miscanthus sinensis
var. *condensatus* 'Cosmopolitan'

VARIEGATED FORMS

Acorus gramineus 'Ogon'
Golden variegated sweet flag

Six- to 12-inch-tall clumps of semi-evergreen to evergreen, bright yellow leaves with some green striping; flowers are insignificant. Light shade; evenly moist soil. *Zones 6 to 10*

Carex morrowii 'Variegata'
Striped sedge

A generic name for all unnamed, striped-edge forms, so plants can be variable. One-foot-tall clumps of narrow green, white-edged leaves that are evergreen in all but the coldest climates. Many other beautiful variegated cultivars are available. Partial shade; takes average garden soil but prefers moist, rich soil. *Zones 5 to 9*

Carex phyllocephala 'Sparkler'
'Sparkler' sedge

Two- to 3-foot-tall clumps of upright to somewhat sprawling, reddish purple stems with whorls of green leaves broadly edged (and sometimes streaked) with creamy white. Clusters of brownish spikes appear at stem tips in summer. Full sun to partial shade; evenly moist, fertile soil. *Zones 8 to 10*

Miscanthus sinensis 'Strictus'
Porcupine grass

Upright, 4- to 6-foot-tall clumps of green leaves with horizontal light yellow bands, turning tan throughout by winter. 'Zebrinus' has more arching foliage. Full sun to light shade; average to evenly moist soil. *Zones 5 to 9*

Miscanthus sinensis
var. *condensatus* 'Cosmopolitan'
'Cosmopolitan' miscanthus

Five- to 6-foot-tall clumps of arching, dark green leaves with cream-to-white edges, turning tan for winter. *M. sinensis* 'Variegatus' has wider white margins but usually needs staking. Full sun or light shade; average to evenly moist, well-drained soil. *Zones 6 to 9*

Phalaris arundinacea 'Dwarf Garters'
Dwarf gardener's garters

Also known as 'Wood's Dwarf'; spreading, 1-foot-tall masses of upright green leaves with vertical white stripes; the leaves and stems often get tinged with pink in spring. Full sun to partial shade; adaptable but prefers evenly moist, fertile soil. *Zones 4 to 9*

A Varied Scene

This sizzling summer combination is both spectacular and practical. By combining eye-catching ornamental foliage with herbs and vegetables, this Seattle garden designed by Steven Antonow provides not only seasonal beauty, but harvest for the table as well.

The brightly variegated golden bamboo (*Pleioblastus viridistriatus*) demands attention as it bursts forth from its less obtrusive companions. On closer inspection, the intricate interplay of foliage textures and colors becomes obvious: the ruby-striped paddles of the canna (*Canna* 'Phaison'), the curiously crinkled kale (*Brassica oleracea*), the glossy dwarf dahlia (*Dahlia* 'Redskin'), and the gray-green lily pad–like foliage of nasturtium (*Tropaeolum majus* 'Apricot Twist'). Later in the season, the rich jewel-toned blooms of canna and nasturtium add color to the scene, but the variegated bamboo remains the star.

If you want to use golden bamboo in a similar display, don't plant it directly in the ground. Left unchecked, it spreads like gangbusters. Fortunately, it grows well in containers, as do all companions shown here, so you could easily replicate this combination on a deck or patio.

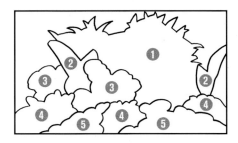

1. *Pleioblastus viridistriatus,* golden bamboo

2. *Canna* 'Phaison', Tropicanna canna

3. *Brassica oleracea,* kale

4. *Dahlia* 'Redskin', 'Redskin' dahlia

5. *Tropaeolum majus,* nasturtium 'Apricot Twist'

Color Surprises

If there's one thing you can expect from grasses, it's the unexpected. You'll get the most enjoyment from these versatile plants if you move beyond fascination with flowers and develop an appreciation for the unique features ornamental grasses offer: interesting foliage, attractive stems, and a range of sometimes unusual flower colors.

Earlier in this chapter, we celebrated the various colored-foliage grasses — gold and bronze, blue and gray, red and black, and variegates — all valuable tools for harmonizing similarly colored companions and for creating arresting accents. Yet another way to enjoy colored-foliage grasses is to use them as complements and foils for nonplant garden features, such as fences, arbors, and statuary. White-striped grasses, such as variegated miscanthus (*Miscanthus sinensis* 'Variegatus'), for example, make striking accom-

This striking garden scheme uses color-wheel opposites, with bright gold-flowered feather reed grass (*Calamagrostis* x *acutiflora* 'Karl Foerster') flanked by rich purple *Vitex* (behind) and lavender (in front).

paniments for white picket fences and deftly echo white trim on houses and outbuildings. If you're more adventurous with your color selections, the possibilities for dramatic contrasts abound. Picture an intricate mosaic birdbath rising up from a bed of black mondo grass (*Ophiopogon planiscapus* 'Nigrescens'), for instance, or a cobalt blue gazing ball nestled in a mass of bright yellow variegated foxtail grass (*Alopecurus pratensis* 'Variegatus'). Even "plain" green grasses can create wondrous effects, as, for example, vivid silhouettes against a white wall or spirited companions for a candy-apple-red footbridge.

Though not showy in the traditional sense, the flower heads and seed heads of grasses should also be considered when planning color effects. Their colors are more muted than those of typical garden flowers, usually in shades of green, tan, brown, and rust, with some pinks, purples, and yellows. The colors tend to change dramatically through the season, as the flower heads transform into seed heads and, again, as the seeds ripen and disperse. Planting grasses where their flowers will be backlit or sidelit by the rising or setting sun allows you to witness the true beauty of their intricate blooms — the low-angled light transforming daytime grays to shining silver, browns to gleaming bronze, and tans to glimmering gold.

The grass stem is a delicate point of interest that can sometimes be overlooked. Because stems are typically covered by foliage, their contribution to the garden as a whole tends to be subtle. But when you start fine-tuning your plantings for elegant color effects, stem color can add an extra level of interest. Take a close look at 'The Blues' little bluestem (*Schizachyrium scoparium* 'The Blues'), for instance, and you'll discover that the stems have alternating blue and pink stripes that are quite appealing. You might accentuate this unexpected color combination by planting this grass behind a clump of autumn crocuses *(Colchicum)* or next to a pink-flowering chrysanthemum or aster. Another grass with interesting stems is 'Superba' large blue fescue (*Festuca amethystina* 'Superba'), which has a distinct purplish pink cast to its slender flower stalks.

Color effects can also be created by playing garden ornaments against dramatic plants. Here, the bright yellow grass is Bowles' golden sedge (*Carex elata* 'Aurea'). The vivid magenta of the cranesbill *(Geranium)* adds to the vibrance of this display.

(Garden of Linda Cochran, Bainbridge Island, Wash.)

The unusual color patterns on the stems of the restio *Elegia capensis* make this plant a real conversation piece. Pick up the hot tones with a bright perennial like the brilliant bloody cranesbill *(Geranium sanguineum)* for a memorable garden scene. (Elisabeth C. Miller Botanical Garden, Seattle)

As we survey beautiful stems, bamboos deserve special mention. Accented by distinct joints along their length, the stems can be bright green, sunny yellow, powder blue, or even jet black. Beautiful as they are, even the most stalwart bamboophile admits that it would be unwise to expect these enthusiastic spreaders to coexist with less vigorous partners. You don't need to forgo growing bamboo completely, however, because many adapt well to life in containers. In confinement, they don't have sufficient room to reach their full glory and they often require frequent division and repotting. In addition, species of bamboo that are vigorous in warm, humid climates can be much slower to spread in the coolest parts of their hardiness range. So if you live in one of these areas, you may be able to grow them directly in the ground and enjoy their colorful stems without worry.

One other group of grasslike plants to consider growing for interesting stems, as well as incredible textures, is the restios. They're not closely related to true grasses — in fact they're in a separate family, called Restionaceae — but like sedges and rushes, restios resemble grasses and can be used in similar ways in the garden.

Restios hail from several areas in the Southern Hemisphere, including Australia and New Zealand, but it's the South African species that seem to be getting the most attention. They vary widely in appearance — some look much like true grasses from a distance, whereas others more closely resemble bamboos or rushes — but they do share the trait of having male and female flowers on separate plants. Their branched or unbranched, upright or arching green stems take care of photosynthesis, and the leaves are reduced to papery bracts in shades of tan, brown, yellow, rust, and near black. Brownish flower clusters appear near the tips of mature stems in summer and can last into winter.

Restios haven't yet been grown widely in the United States, so we're still learning about their preferred growing conditions and hardiness. Current thinking is that most are hardy only south of Zone 7, but as more gardeners experiment with them, we may find they are hardier. Similarly, it was once assumed that restios required full sun and dry, well-drained soil, but many are adapting well to a wider range of garden conditions.

In addition to making great container plants, restios are excellent for adding color and texture to landscapes, either alone as specimens or combined with companions in beds and borders.

WORKING WITH COLOR

Alopecurus pratensis 'Variegatus'

Alopecurus pratensis 'Variegatus'
Variegated foxtail grass
One-foot-tall tufts of narrow, bright green leaves with yellow vertical stripes, or all-yellow leaves. Color is best in cool weather; cut back by half or slightly more when the flowers appear for fresh foliage by fall. Full sun to light shade; evenly moist soil.
Zones 5 to 8

Eragrostis spectabilis
Purple love grass
Mounds of fine-textured, green foliage to about 18 inches tall; flowers are clouds of branched, reddish purple panicles in late summer. May be short lived but self-sows freely. Full sun; average, well-drained soil.
Zones 5 to 9

Pennisetum alopecuroides 'Moudry'
'Moudry' fountain grass
Dense, 2-foot-tall mounds of arching, glossy green leaves that usually turn yellow or orange in fall. Three-foot-tall stems rise in late summer to early fall, topped with fluffy, spikelike flower clusters that are dark reddish purple to near black. Self-sowing. Full sun to light shade; best in evenly moist, well-drained soil but adaptable.
Zones 6 to 9

Phormium tenax
New Zealand flax
Clumps of swordlike, evergreen leaves that normally range anywhere from 2 to 4 feet tall. An abundance of cultivars come in a wide range of colors and combinations, including the classic yellow-and-green 'Yellow Wave' and the moody, deep purple 'Platt's Black'. Compact 'Duet', with gold-and-green leaves, stays about 2 feet tall. *Phormium cookianum* 'Flamingo' offers olive green leaves with incredible pink and coral striping. Great in containers. Full sun; average, well-drained soil. *Zones 8 to 10*

Themeda japonica
Japanese themeda
Broad clumps of fuzzy, 3- to 4-foot-tall stems with bright green leaves that turn an amazing reddish orange in fall and hold their coppery tones well into winter. Full sun; average, well-drained soil.
Zones 4 to 9

Eragrostis spectabilis

Phormium 'Duet'

A Taste of the Exotic

This extraordinary combination from the Strybing Arboretum in San Francisco is an excellent example of dramatic textures, as well as outstanding color effects. At first glance, it's the red-and-green striped blades of 'Maori Maiden' New Zealand flax (*Phormium* 'Maori Maiden') that draw our eyes to the middle of the border. To either side, the rich green saw palmetto *(Serenoa repens)* and silvery blue yucca *(Yucca* sp.) provide both a contrast of color and an echo of texture. The lighter green grass *(Anemanthele lessoniana)* in the foreground and cannomois *(Cannomois virgata)* at the right serve a similar function, but with a twist — notice how the reddish bracts on the cannomois stems pick up the brighter red of the flax foliage.

Don't count on these plants being hardy north of Zone 8. In colder areas, you might find it worth the work to grow them in pots and bring them indoors for winter; otherwise, you'll need to choose similar-looking but hardier replacements. The most challenging part would be finding something similar to the exotic-looking cannomois. A red-twigged dogwood *(Cornus alba)* might do the trick for the red echo, and the cultivar 'Gouchaultii', with green leaves splashed with pink and yellow, would add even more interest to the mix.

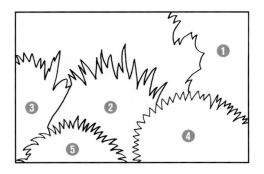

1. *Cannomois virgata,* cannomois

2. *Phormium* 'Maori Maiden', 'Maori Maiden' New Zealand flax

3. *Serenoa repens,* saw palmetto

4. *Yucca* sp., yucca

5. *Anemanthele lessoniana,* pheasant's-tail grass

YEARLONG BEAUTY

ABOVE: A pastel combination in early summer features roses, dogwood, Japanese silver grass (*Miscanthus sinensis* 'Morning Light'), and other perennials.

OPPOSITE: Both the texture and rich color of the foliage and flowers of purple fountain grass (*Pennisetum setaceum* 'Rubrum') work especially well with the pink *Cleome* and scarlet bee balm (*Monarda didyma*) in this summer flower border.

Grasses hold potential for enlivening each part of your landscape, from adding substance to beds and borders to creating a dramatic garden accent. Once you appreciate their adaptability, you'll discover that even demure grasses can make a memorable statement.

Ornamental grasses come in all shapes and sizes, making it easy to find one suitable for any spot. For example, low-growing dwarf copper sedge *(Carex berggrenii)* is a compact clump-former, just right to liven up a tiny corner, whereas giant reed *(Arundo donax)* is an imposing spreader, perfect for filling space in a large landscape. Because grasses of all sizes can adapt beautifully to life in containers, even gardeners with minimal space can enjoy their colors, texture, movement, and sounds. In water gardens, nothing can surpass the texture of sweet flag (*Acorus* spp.) or the unusual whorled foliage of umbrella sedge *(Cyperus alternifolius)* as a delicate complement to the bold and beautiful blooms of water lilies and lotuses.

As you become acquainted with the many different ornamental grasses available and observe how they can be combined with other garden plants, you'll want to experiment with ways to incorporate them into your own garden and landscape designs. In this chapter, we'll explore some of the diverse landscape areas that make perfect settings for grasses and demonstrate ways to use these versatile plants for both sculptural interest and points of color throughout the year.

A New Twist on Beds and Borders

Move over, perennials and annuals; ornamental grasses are now holding court in beds and borders. Recognizing that grasses are far more than space fillers, adventurous gardeners are designing grasses into their borders from the outset, and the results, though sometimes unexpected, are always spectacular.

BEYOND BEAUTY

Artistic considerations aside, there are also excellent practical reasons to consider adding ornamental grasses to your borders.

• Warm-season grasses wait until the weather starts heating up to put on most of their growth, so they're ideal for filling spaces left when spring bulbs and early-flowering perennials go dormant in early- to midsummer.

• Sturdy grasses can help minimize staking chores because they'll mingle with and support weaker-stemmed partners in a way that's as alluring as it is labor-saving.

• Low to medium-height grasses are perfect companions for covering the "bare ankles" of taller-growing perennials that tend to lose their lower leaves as the season progresses — including bee balm (*Monarda* spp.) and border phlox (*Phlox paniculata*), to name just two.

Ornamental grasses come in a wide range of heights, so there's a perfect choice for any spot from the front edge to the very back of the border. Another obvious consideration for garden design is color, and here you can use grasses to your advantage in several ways. If you need a dependable, even-toned foil behind more airy flowering plants, dense clumps of green-leaved grasses make a handsome backdrop for pale or wispy blooms, such as airy white gaura *(Gaura lindheimeri)*, pale yellow scabious (*Scabiosa ochroleuca*), and steel-blue globe thistles *(Echinops ritro),* which can easily get lost against a less distinct background. Green grasses also work well for separating strong colors and boldly patterned blooms, such as the intense red heads of Maltese cross *(Lychnis chalcedonica)* and the bull's-eye stripes of blanket flower *(Gaillardia* x *grandiflora).* Grass foliage makes its own color contribution to the border, and it's hard not to be tempted by the surprising variety of foliage color choices, from yellow, red, and orange, to brown, blue, or even multihued. Gold, silver, copper, or bronze flower clusters and seed heads, when caught by light, cast an almost metallic sheen over the entire garden setting.

Beyond color, grasses have other assets to offer beds and borders — most notably,

form and texture. A fair number of traditional border denizens possess distinct upright or mounded forms, making the arching habits of many grasses a welcome transition between the two. And when you consider the dramatic contrast of fine-textured grasses against the bold foliage of hostas, heucheras, and cannas — to name just a few broad-leaved border favorites — it's easy to see that possibilities for outstanding combinations abound.

A subtler benefit comes from a less tangible quality of most grasses, and it may be the best of all the contributions grasses make to a bed or border: they add a softer, more natural feel to even the most precisely planned plantings, evoking the free-for-all charm of a flower-studded meadow while maintaining the tidiness and balance of a carefully cultivated border.

As they mature, ornamental grasses provide exciting changes throughout the summer months just when most borders

RIGHT: Simple, yet bold, this border features the upright California rush *Juncus patens* 'Carman's Gray' in company with Japanese maple *(Acer palmatum),* an ornamental onion (*Allium* 'Globe-master'), and veronica (*Veronica* 'Trehane'). (Garden of Linda Cochran, Bainbridge Island, Wash.)

CORRALLING CREEPING GRASSES

Green-and-white-striped gardener's garters (*Phalaris arundinacea* 'Picta') and blue-green Lyme grass *(Leymus arenarius)* are undeniably enticing when controlled at the nursery. But bring these beauties home and release them in your borders, and you'll be sorry! The adage is all too true: "The first year, they sleep; the second year, they creep; and the third year, they leap."

To enjoy these spreaders without worry, plant them in pots or bottomless buckets, then sink the containers almost to their rim in your bed or border. Leave about 1 inch of pot rim above the soil surface to help discourage the runners from climbing out over the top. This approach isn't foolproof, so it's wise to check for escapees on a regular basis. When the pot gets crowded, simply divide the plants, replant just one small piece per pot, and you're in business again.

shine, but they're interesting at unexpected times, too. The fall foliage colors of warm-season grasses, for instance, can rival some of the showiest deciduous shrubs and trees. Their winter colors are more muted, but the russets, golds, and tans are still welcome, as are the persistent seed heads that transform snow and ice into ever-changing winter sculptures. Cool-season grasses, too, shine during the colder months, bridging the gap between the last of the fall-flowering perennials and the earliest spring bulbs.

When choosing grasses for beds and borders, keep in mind their relative tendencies to creep or self-sow. There are some truly beautiful creeping grasses, but unless you're prepared to contain them at planting time, you may rue the day you ever let them loose in your border.

Clump-formers and slow spreaders are less likely to crowd out bed and border companions, but some multiply almost as rapidly because they are overly generous with their seed production, leaving you with a dilemma: do you cut off the seed heads in fall and lose their winter show, or let them stand and deal with weeding out the unwanted seedlings the following year? In established beds and borders, you can probably get away with the latter approach because there's not much bare

soil for the seeds to drop into, and adding a fresh layer of mulch each spring can keep volunteers to a minimum. But in a newer landscape with lots of exposed soil, removing the seed heads in fall might be a better option.

Most ornamental grasses adapt readily to the same growing conditions that typical border plants appreciate: full sun to light shade, and well-drained soil that doesn't dry out completely. Nutrient needs, however, differ. While traditional wisdom calls for frequent applications of fertilizer to keep border perennials blooming, overly fertile soil can lead to too-lush, floppy growth in grasses. For new gardens, rather than enriching the soil in the whole bed before planting, one way to address the problem is to add soil amendments to the individual holes where you plant perennials but no fertilizer where you plant grasses. During the subsequent growing seasons, you might consider using a compost mulch in spring, with fewer or lighter feedings in summer, or no additional fertilizer at all. Of course, you could also fertilize the perennials as usual and simply stake your grasses, or shear them back in early summer to promote more compact regrowth; it all depends on how much additional work you want to do.

Festuca idahoensis 'Siskiyou Blue'

DESIGNER'S CHOICE

BEDS AND BORDERS

Carex dolichostachya 'Kaga Nishiki' (Gold Fountains sedge)

One-foot-tall mounds of slender, arching green leaves edged with gold; evergreen except in coldest parts of its range; early summer flowers are inconspicuous purplish spikes. Sun to partial shade; fertile, evenly moist soil. *Zones 5 or 6 to 9*

Elymus magellanicus Magellan wheatgrass

Dense, 1-foot-tall clumps of silvery blue foliage with wheatlike spikes of blue-green flowers atop 18-inch stems in early summer. Full sun; and average, well-drained soil. *Zones 5 to 9*

Festuca idahoensis 'Siskiyou Blue' 'Siskiyou Blue' Idaho fescue

Six- to 8-inch-tall tufts of bright silvery blue leaves. Blue-green to tan flower panicles bloom atop 1-foot-tall stems in early summer. Full sun to light shade; average to dry, well-drained soil. *Zones 5 to 9*

Miscanthus sinensis 'Gracillimus' Maiden grass

Dense, 5- to 6-foot-tall clumps of narrow, arching green leaves with orange, yellow, or brown fall color, then tan in winter; many-branched, reddish brown flower clusters appear atop 6- to 7-foot-tall stems in mid- to late fall (none in cool climates), then turn silvery white and last into winter. Full sun; average to evenly moist, well-drained soil. *Zones 5 to 9*

Miscanthus sinensis 'Morning Light' 'Morning Light' miscanthus

Four- to 5-foot-tall clumps of slender, white-edged green, upright-to-arching leaves. Branched flower clusters bloom well over the foliage on 5- to 6-foot stems, starting reddish brown in late summer to early fall, then turning creamy white. Full sun to light shade; average to evenly moist, well-drained soil. *Zones 5 to 9*

Miscanthus sinensis 'Gracillimus'

Miscanthus sinensis 'Morning Light'

AN ELEGANT BORDER

This exquisite border at Heronswood Nursery in Kingston, Washington, is a study in early summer color, but thanks to a well-chosen grass, it remains beautiful even while the flowers are taking a break. Golden Hakone grass (*Hakonechloa macra* 'Aureola') offers slowly expanding mounds of bright yellow leaves lightly striped with green — a charming complement to bright blue 'Bill Baker' forget-me-nots (*Myosotis scorpioides* 'Bill Baker'), purple 'Nimbus' geranium (*Geranium* 'Nimbus'), and silvery lamb's ears *(Stachys byzantina)*. A single clump makes an eye-catching accent, but the repetition of this grass's distinctive color and flowing form provides a predictable unity and appealing rhythm to the border all season long.

Hardy in Zones 5 to 9, golden Hakone grass can take full sun in cool, moist climates; elsewhere, it appreciates light shade. In any climate, evenly moist, humus-rich soil is best. A wide range of popular border perennials thrive in the same conditions, so it's a simple matter to tailor this theme to suit your favorite flower colors.

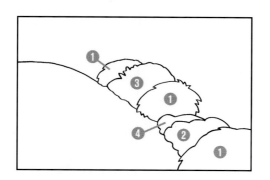

1. *Hakonechloa macra* 'Aureola', golden Hakone grass
2. *Myosotis scorpioides* 'Bill Baker', 'Bill Baker' forget-me-nots
3. *Geranium* 'Nimbus', 'Nimbus' geranium
4. *Stachys byzantina*, lamb's ears

FRONT YARD GARDENS

If you're bored with a predictable foundation planting, consider adding ornamental grasses to your front garden. Easy-care and dependable, grasses provide seasonal interest, along with color, height, and texture. As an added bonus, the soft, distinctive rustle of the grass leaves helps filter any noises from the street.

THE PUBLIC SPACE

Before you decide to replace your entire front yard with grasses, consider the overall character of your neighborhood. In a traditional suburban neighborhood with formal, evergreen foundation plantings, you might want to begin using ornamental grasses fairly conservatively — perhaps starting with a single accent of *Miscanthus,* then gradually working additional grasses into your plantings. If your neighbors have varied plantings, you can be more adventurous with your planting schemes. Of course, if you're miles from your nearest neighbor, you're free to do whatever you like best.

Choose grasses that are in proportion to your house and the rest of your landscape. A towering clump of giant reed (*Arundo donax*) is dramatic in some settings but can be overpowering in small areas. Also, consider the shape of the grasses. Those like maiden grass (*Miscanthus sinensis* 'Gracillimus'), with distinct forms, may be perceived as less radical than more casual grasses, like tufted hair grass (*Deschampsia cespitosa*).

Compared to the usual globe- and cube-shaped, sheared evergreens that routinely serve as foundation plantings, ornamental grasses offer a softer, more natural form that artfully conceals and blends the hard edges of your home into the surrounding landscape. Grasses also ease the transition between highly manicured plantings of shrubs and perennials and the clipped lawn beyond.

If your property includes a strip of lawn between the sidewalk and the street, consider planting low-growing, low-maintenance ornamental grasses — a tremendous improvement over an uninteresting strip of turf grass that's difficult to mow and takes forever to trim. Before growing ornamental grasses in the strip between sidewalk and street, however, check with your local zoning board to find out whether there are any restrictions regarding the planting and maintenance of that area.

Front-yard plantings need to look great year-round, so select grasses that have a long season of interest. And, for such public areas, it's particularly important to avoid using grasses that spread quickly by runners or by self-sown seedlings. Your neighbors are likely to be unhappy if your grasses start to pop up unexpectedly in their yards.

ABOVE: This exuberant sidewalk garden in Seattle fills both the front yard and the curbside strip with a subtle tapestry of perennials and ornamental grasses.

OPPOSITE: Repeated clumps of pheasant's-tail grass (*Anemanthele lessoniana),* blue fescue (*Festuca glauca),* and large blue fescue (*Festuca amethystina)* share the public space with *Salvia officinalis* 'Purpurea' and other ground covers.

Miscanthus sinensis 'Adagio'

Cortaderia selloana 'Pumila'

Calamagrostis x *acutiflora* 'Karl Foerster'

FRONT YARDS

Calamagrostis x *acutiflora* 'Karl Foerster'
'Karl Foerster' feather reed grass

Clumps of shiny, deep green leaves to 3 feet tall; slender pinkish plumes bloom above the foliage on 4- to 6-foot stems in early summer and last through most of the winter. Full sun; takes average soil but prefers moist, fertile conditions. *Zones 5 to 9*

Cortaderia selloana 'Pumila'
Dwarf pampas grass

Compact, 3-foot-tall, evergreen clumps of arching, green foliage; creamy white flower plumes freely produced atop 4- to 6-foot-tall stems in late summer. Full sun to light shade; adaptable but best in fertile, evenly moist soil. *Zones 7 to 10*

Festuca glauca 'Elijah Blue'
'Elijah Blue' fescue

Dense, 6-inch-tall tufts of bright silvery blue foliage; flowers are blue-green panicles on 10-inch-tall stems in early summer, turning tan. Full sun; average, well-drained soil. *Zones 4 to 8*

Miscanthus sinensis 'Adagio'
'Adagio' miscanthus

Compact, 2- to 3-foot-tall mounds of arching, narrow, grayish green leaves that turn yellow in fall; branched flower clusters atop 4- to 5-foot stems are pink-tinged tan in late summer, aging to silvery tan. Full sun to light shade; average to evenly moist, well-drained soil. *Zones 5 or 6 to 9*

Pennisetum alopecuroides 'Hameln'
'Hameln' fountain grass

Dense, 2-foot-tall mounds of arching, narrow, rich green, glossy leaves that turn golden to orange-yellow in fall, then tan for winter; fluffy, upright to arching, spikelike clusters of greenish cream or pinkish flowers bloom atop 3-foot-tall stems in early to midsummer, turning tan and lasting into fall. Full sun (light shade if hot); best in evenly moist, well-drained soil but adaptable to other sites. *Zones 4 to 9*

Featuring Foliage

A color-packed perennial border like this one at Noerenberg Park, Minnetonka, Minnesota, beckons visitors to your front yard. More than a pretty garden, it's also an outstanding example of good design. Notice how the repeated clumps of upright, bright red Japanese blood grass (*Imperata cylindrica* var. *koenigii* 'Red Baron') draw your eye forward, providing a sense of rhythm and continuity, while the varied companions (*Gaura lindheimeri* and *Artemisia* 'Powis Castle' directly behind the blood grass) punctuate the display, offering much to admire along the pathway.

If you find the blood grass too bold, simply replace it with another medium-height grass. Repeated clumps of spiky blue oat grass *(Helictotrichon sempervirens)*, for instance, would look marvelous with silvery foliage and white, pink, and blue flowers while providing an equally striking textural contrast.

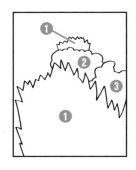

1. *Imperata cylindrica var. koenigii* 'Red Baron', Japanese blood grass

2. *Gaura lindheimeri*, gaura

3. *Artemisia* 'Powis Castle', 'Powis Castle' artemisia

LINING THE PATH

Nothing can turn a stretch of paving into a welcoming walkway as easily as an elegant edging of ornamental grass. The flowing foliage helps soften the abrupt transition between paving and the plantings or lawn beyond, and most grasses are tough enough to withstand being trodden on or trampled occasionally.

Alternating golden Hakone grass (*Hakonechloa macra* 'Aureola') and lady's mantle (*Alchemilla mollis*) are dependable path brighteners.

When selecting grasses for planting along a path or walkway, seek out species that aren't too tall: 2 feet or less in height is ideal. In high-traffic areas, low-growing grasses clearly define a path's route, naturally directing visitors and allowing them to see where they are going. Taller grasses create a more closed-in effect, which can be fanciful and fun along a lesser-used garden path but would be unwelcoming in a walkway used by visitors to your home.

Once you have determined the height that will be best for a particular spot, you can narrow down your grass options based on the effect you wish to create. You'll want heavily used paths to look their best year-round, so for those locales select grasses that have multi-season interest: handsome foliage at least, and perhaps pretty seed heads, showy fall color, and good winter structure. Warm-season grasses will have some down time in late winter and early spring once you've cut them back, but you can fill that gap in the show beautifully with spring-flowering bulbs. By the time the bulb foliage starts to die back, the grasses will begin filling in, concealing the yellowing bulb leaves.

Grasses with interesting details work well along less-used paths, where a meandering visitor can stroll slowly, stopping to admire individual plants. For instance, you might line a path with the curious one-sided blooms of blue grama grass (*Bouteloua gracilis*), the fuzzy, tufted flowers of annual hare's tail grass (*Lagurus ovatus*), or 'Fairy's Joke' tufted hair grass (*Deschampsia cespitosa* 'Fairy's Joke'), which produces tiny grass plantlets where the blooms would normally form. Ground-hugging dwarf Japanese sweet flag (*Acorus gramineus* 'Pusillus') makes a wonderful accent when planted along and between stepping-stones, because the foliage releases a light spicy-sweet fragrance when you tread on it.

When you plant grasses along a walkway, set them back so they will just cover the path's edge when fully grown; don't place them right next to the paving. Even with proper positioning and spacing, it's best to avoid using sharp-leaved grasses, such as pampas grass (*Cortaderia selloana*) and prairie cord grass (*Spartina pectinata*), where unsuspecting passersby could accidentally brush against them.

Paved surfaces radiate lots of heat and reflect light onto nearby plantings, so unless your path is in the shade, choose sun-loving, heat-tolerant grasses, which may require some supplemental water under certain conditions. If you live in a cold-winter climate, consider salt-tolerant grasses for paved paths where you use rock salt to help melt ice and snow.

Finally, if you plan to plant creeping or self-sowing grasses along paths that have unmortared joints — for example, along paths of bricks or pavers set in sand, rather than cement — beware! Cracks can provide ideal points of entry for seedlings and runners, which will give your walkway a weedy appearance and considerably increase the time needed for your maintenance chores. Sinking a metal or plastic edging strip along the sides of the path before planting the grasses will help to keep creepers out, and removing seed heads will reduce or eliminate self-sown seedlings.

This colorful edging juxtaposes the neutral gold tones of 'Hameln' fountain grass (*Pennisetum alopecuroides* 'Hameln') with the vibrant purple of floss flower (*Ageratum houstonianum*) and the deeper tones of purple-leaved beefsteak plant (*Perilla frutescens* 'Atropurpurea'). (Chanticleer Garden, Wayne, Penn.)

Carex tumulicola

Festuca amethystina 'Superba'

Luzula sylvatica 'Aurea'

PATHS AND WALKWAYS

Carex tumulicola
Berkeley sedge
Spreading evergreen mounds of slender, arching, deep green leaves that are usually 12 to 18 inches tall. Brownish flowers appear in spring. Full sun to shade; prefers evenly moist soil but has some drought tolerance when established. *Zones 8 to 10*

Deschampsia cespitosa 'Fairy's Joke'
'Fairy's Joke' tufted hair grass
Also known as *Deschampsia cespitosa* var. *vivipara,* 2- to 3-foot-tall clumps of spiky to arching dark green leaves; evergreen except in coldest zones; in late spring to early summer, 3- to 5-foot-tall, arching stems bear loose, airy panicles with small greenish yellow plantlets instead of seeds, turning tan later. Light shade; evenly moist but well-drained, fertile soil. *Zones 4 to 9*

Festuca amethystina 'Superba'
'Superba' large blue fescue
Dense, 1-foot-tall tufts of fine-textured, blue-green foliage; flowers are narrow, bluish to purplish green panicles atop 2-foot-tall stems in late spring to early summer, turning tan. Full sun (light shade in hot areas); average, well-drained soil. *Zones 4 to 8*

Lagurus ovatus
Hare's tail grass
Six- to 8-inch-tall tufts of soft, light green leaves; upright, 12- to 18-inch-tall stems tipped with fuzzy, dense, oval panicles that start out green and then turn white. Full sun; average, well-drained soil. *Annual*

Luzula sylvatica
Greater woodrush
Moderately spreading, 1-foot-tall carpets of bright to medium green, glossy leaves with fine hairs; evergreen in mild climates; airy, light green to brown flowers on 2-foot-tall stems in spring. The cultivar 'Aurea' has yellow-green leaves. Partial shade; prefers moist soil but drought tolerant. *Zones 4 to 9*

A Study in Darks and Lights

A lightly shaded garden path lined with a tapestry of multihued and variously textured foliage — such as this clever combination of black mondo grass (*Ophiopogon planiscapus* 'Nigrescens') and 'Gold Band' sedge (*Carex morrowii* 'Gold Band') with ferny-leaved wild bleeding heart (*Dicentra* sp.), scallop-edged columbine (*Aquilegia* sp.), and other perennials at Plant Delights Nursery, Raleigh, North Carolina — provides an intricate display that encourages passersby to pause and admire.

A pathway planting that relies primarily on foliage, rather than flowers, has the advantage of long-lasting appeal,

an important consideration for an oft-traveled walkway. Better still, with no blooms to attract pollinating bees, this planting offers no hazards to those who prefer to keep bees at a distance.

Black mondo grass is a particularly good choice for pathway plantings such as this, as it tends to get "lost" against soil and mulch when seen from a distance. When set off with bright-leaved sedge, as it is here, black mondo grass comes into its own. After the other perennials die back for winter, the evergreen mondo grass and sedge remain, providing welcome interest during the off-season.

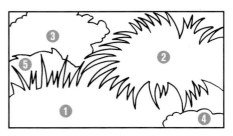

1. *Ophiopogon planiscapus* 'Nigrescens', black mondo grass

2. *Carex morrowii* 'Gold Band' 'Gold Band' sedge

3. *Dicentra* sp., bleeding heart

4. *Aquilegia* sp., columbine

5. Fern

Perfect for Pots

Perhaps somewhat surprisingly, grasses make excellent additions to pots, planters, and window boxes of all sizes. As well as adding multiseason interest to decks, patios, and other areas, growing grasses in containers gives you freedom to experiment with species that may not be suitable for your beds and borders.

When you're putting together container plantings, it's easy to find options for bushy and trailing flowers and foliage. The tricky part is finding good-looking upright plants to add height. An ornamental grass may be the perfect solution. Young plants of even the tallest grasses make striking vertical accents in container combinations. Look for foliage in a wide array of colors, not to mention the interesting flowers and showy fall foliage that come as an added bonus.

Pots and planters are also wonderful for showcasing the cascading foliage of grasses having fountainlike or arching forms. And because container plantings generally reside closer to eye level than garden plantings, they're ideal for grasses with subtle variegation or delicate flowers that demand a second look.

Growing grasses in pots can be aesthetically pleasing and surprisingly prac-

TOP: A dramatic focal point, container-grown pampas grass (Cortaderia selloana) is surrounded by a colorful carpet of 'Tiger Eyes' marigolds and 'Ogon' spirea. (Chanticleer Garden, Wayne, Penn.)

BOTTOM: Golden Hakone grass (Hakonechloa macra 'Aureola') shares a container with begonias and variegated flowering maple (Abutilon megapotamicum 'Variegatum').

tical, too. If you can't afford large slow-growing grasses, or you get a mail-order delivery of grasses that are too small to go directly into your garden, a wonderful interim solution is to grow them in pots and enjoy them on your deck or patio for a few years, then plant them out when they're large enough to hold their own in the open garden.

Pots and planters make it possible for cooler-climate gardeners to enjoy grasses that wouldn't otherwise survive winter, such as New Zealand flax (Phormium tenax). True, you can plant tender grasses in the ground and dig them up each year, but over time, managing those clumps can become rather cumbersome. Keeping them in smaller pots makes moving them indoors for the winter a much simpler proposition, especially when early frosts threaten.

Most important, perhaps, containers give you an opportunity to grow grasses that you might otherwise not choose to let loose in your garden soil. Many beautiful bamboos, for example, can be terrors in the open garden, sending runners out many yards from their point of origin. But put them in a sturdy pot on your patio, and voilà: you can enjoy them without a second thought. The same is true for grasses that have fast-spreading roots, such as giant blue wild rye *(Leymus racemosus)*. The container confines the roots to one spot, forcing the plant to produce a handsome, bushy clump, rather than scattered, unexpected sprigs throughout the garden.

The growing medium you use for other container plantings will be adequate for most ornamental grasses. You might want to add sand or perlite, and an inch or so of gravel as a top-dressing, for grasses that demand good drainage or more peat moss for grasses that appreciate extra moisture. Setting a saucer under the pot and keeping it filled with water can also help to keep the soil damp for moisture-loving grasses.

The size of the pot you use depends on the particular grass you're growing and what, if anything, you'll be planting with it. Upright grasses are exceptional companions for lower-growing flowering and foliage plants in large planters, while fountainlike grasses do well when planted in smaller pots and allowed to cascade freely.

In this elegant container, white-and-green variegated Japanese silver grass (*Miscanthus sinensis* 'Cosmopolitan') combines with scarlet *Phygelius* x *rectus* and a rosy *Geranium* cultivar. (Elisabeth C. Miller Botanical Garden, Seattle)

Phormium cookianum 'Flamingo'

Ophiopogon planiscapus 'Nigrescens'

Bromus inermis 'Skinner's Gold'

POTS AND PLANTERS

Bromus inermis 'Skinner's Gold'
Skinner's gold brome
Fast-spreading masses of 2- to 3-foot-tall, yellow stems with yellow-striped green leaves; flowers are airy tan panicles atop the stems in midsummer. Full sun; average to moist, well-drained soil. *Zones 5 to 8 (possibly colder)*

Cyperus papyrus
Papyrus
Upright, smooth, stout stems usually 4 to 6 feet tall, topped with clusters of narrow green bracts; showy clusters of greenish to brownish flowers through summer. Full sun to partial shade; needs constant moisture and grows in water to about 3 feet deep. *Zones 9 to 10 (elsewhere, overwinter indoors)*

Isolepis cernua
Mop sedge, fiber optics grass
Also known as *Elocharis cernuus* or *Scirpus cernuus*; dense, 6- to 12-inch-tall mounds of arching, bright green, fine-textured stems; evergreen in Zone 10. Stems are tipped with white to brownish spikes that last into winter. Full sun to light shade; needs ample moisture or shallow water. *Zones 8 to 10*

Leymus arenarius
Lyme grass
Also known as *Elymus arenarius* 'Glaucus' or *Elymus glaucus*; 1- to 2-foot-tall, blue-green, sharp-edged, arching leaves; deciduous in cold climates. Narrow, bluish green flower spikes sporadic through summer. Full sun to light shade; drought-tolerant. *Zones 4 to 10*

Ophiopogon planiscapus 'Nigrescens'
Black mondo grass
Slow-spreading, 6- to 8-inch-tall, evergreen clumps of narrow, grasslike, near-black leaves. Full sun to partial shade; average to moist soil. *Zones 6 to 10*

Phormium cookianum 'Flamingo'
'Flamingo' New Zealand flax
Showy evergreen, 3-foot-tall clumps of swordlike, olive green leaves striped with varying amounts of pink, peach, and coral. Full sun; average, well-drained soil. *Zones 8 to 10*

Designing for an Urn

Overflowing with New Zealand flax (*Phormium tenax*) and other colorful companions, this striking urn at Montrose Garden, Durham, North Carolina, is both exuberant and elegant. The burgundy-leaved coleus (*Solenostemon* sp.) complements the moody hues of the New Zealand flax and the container itself, while the white-and-green coleus and pale yellow lantana (*Lantana* sp.) serve as vibrant accents that visually link the planter with the surrounding borders.

Containers like this one invite creativity and experimentation. Combine grasses and companion plants that you think will work well together, then see what you think. If you're not pleased with the results, simply replace some of the plants to fine-tune the effect, move the container to a less visible spot, or resolve to try a different combination next year.

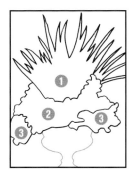

1. *Phormium tenax*, New Zealand flax
2. *Solenostemon* sp., coleus
3. *Lantana* sp., lantana

Companions for Roses

Perennials, annuals, bulbs, and shrubs all make fitting companions for grasses. But what about roses? Certainly, roses are not often paired with grasses, for reasons that we'll soon address. But if you enjoy growing grasses and love raising roses, finding a way for them to thrive together is a logical next step.

The main reservation some gardeners have about growing grasses with roses is a practical one: grasses and roses prefer different growing conditions. Grasses have a reputation for laughing at drought and favoring lean soil, whereas roses are traditionally pampered with regular irrigation and generous applications of fertilizer. Though this may be true, it is possible to create a happy medium where both plants perform well. The majority of roses and grasses thrive in full sun, and that's half the battle; it's far easier to modify a fertilization and watering program than it is to change a garden's light levels.

Drought tolerance is a trait shared by many grasses, but that doesn't necessarily mean they require dry soil. A more generous moisture supply can encourage taller, lusher-looking grass growth (taller and bushier than books suggest) and help some shade-requiring grasses tolerate more sunlight.

Another factor that can encourage particularly vigorous growth in grasses is an abundance of nutrients, especially nitrogen. When pairing roses with grasses, you may want to consider cutting back on the amount you fertilize your roses to keep the neighboring grasses from getting too big. To ensure adequate nutrients, but at a slower rate, enrich the soil with organic matter (not quick-release chemical materials) *before* planting to encourage more balanced growth.

You can spring-prune roses and cut down warm-season grasses at the same time. Dividing grasses, particularly those growing close to the roses, is more challenging, so position plants with this in mind. Also, think twice about combining roses with grasses that spread quickly by runners or by self-sowing, unless you're willing to plant runners in root barriers and deadhead the self-sowers.

The sensuous informality of this peony-like rose almost seems to challenge the preppy stripes of 'Cosmopolitan' miscanthus (*Miscanthus sinensis* var. *condensatus* 'Cosmopolitan'). (Freeland Tanner garden, Napa, Calif.)

If you enjoy color and textural contrasts in your garden, you may prize the juxtaposition of fine-textured grass foliage and bold, velvety rose blooms. Grasses soften hard edges and help rose plants blend more seamlessly into mixed plantings. Lower, mounding grasses help hide the "bare ankles" of roses, and the arching foliage of taller grasses mingles with and hides the roses' angular canes. Rich green grass foliage can also differentiate the vibrant hues of brightly colored roses from one another, helping them to blend into the border.

You may find a "wild" single-flowered rose a more appropriate partner for your favorite grass. Select species roses or a large-flowered but single hybrid such as the soft pink hybrid tea 'Dainty Bess', bright pink floribunda 'Betty Prior', or yellow shrub 'Golden Wings'. The small-scale single, semidouble, or fully double blooms of miniature roses are often just the right scale for grasses' slender leaves and delicate flowers.

When choosing a grass-rose combination, note that cool-season grasses tend to reach their peak at about the same time that roses are in their full glory, so your garden will look truly spectacular in late spring and early summer. For the midsummer period when most roses take a break before reblooming, use warm-season grasses, which put on lots of leafy

An inviting, luxurious border features 'Golden Wings' and 'Graham Thomas' roses along with blue oat grass (Helictotrichon sempervirens), Mexican feather grass (Nassella tenuissima), and toe toe (Cortaderia richardii).

growth during the warm weather; those with variegated or colored foliage provide plenty of interest and visual excitement even when flowers are few. Late summer and fall bring warm-season grasses into bloom and develop their vibrant fall colors, just in time to harmonize with the late reblooming roses and ripening rose hips.

Miscanthus sinensis var. *condensatus*
'Cosmopolitan'

Cortaderia richardii

Miscanthus sinensis 'Variegatus'

ROSE COMPANIONS

Carex oshimensis 'Evergold'
'Evergold' sedge

Also known as *Carex hachijoensis* 'Evergold'; dense, 12- to 18-inch-tall mounds of arching, narrow leaves that are glossy green with a cream to yellow center stripe, which appears all yellow from a distance. Early spring flowers are brownish spikes, not showy. Prefers light shade (such as under shrubs); evenly moist soil. *Zones 6 to 8*

Cortaderia spp.
Pampas grasses

Large, clump-forming grasses with arching foliage and 6- to 12-foot-tall stems topped with dramatic flower plumes toward summer's end. *Cortaderia selloana* is the most readily available species; there are many cultivars. *Cortaderia richardii* (commonly called toe toe) is an evergreen species that usually reaches about 8 feet in bloom, with gently arching, creamy white flower plumes. *Zones 7 or 8 to 10*

Cymbopogon citratus
Lemon grass

Dense clumps of upright, greenish to purple-tinted stems, with light green leaves that are strongly lemon-scented. Height usually 2 to 3 feet; seldom flowers. Enjoy it as an added source of fragrance with roses. Full sun to light shade; adaptable but prefers moist, well drained soil. *Zones 9 and 10; elsewhere, overwinter indoors*

Festuca amethystina 'Superba'
'Superba' large blue fescue

Also known as *Festuca glauca* 'Superba'; 10-inch-tall tufts of fine-textured, blue-green foliage. Late-spring to early-summer flowers are narrow, bluish to purplish green panicles on purplish pink, 18- to 20-inch-tall stems. Full sun (or light shade in hot areas); average, well-drained soil. *Zones 4 to 8*

Miscanthus sinensis 'Variegatus'
Variegated miscanthus

Loose, 5- to 6-foot-tall clumps of arching, bright green leaves with broad white vertical stripes. Red-tinged silver flower clusters on 6- to 8-foot stems turn tan in early fall. *Miscanthus sinensis* var. *condensatus* 'Cosmopolitan' has dark green leaves with cream-to-white edges; does not need staking. Full sun; average to evenly moist, well-drained soil. *Zones 6 to 9*

A Lavish Border with Roses

Captured here in its late spring abundance, the ethereal 'Bonica' rose (*Rosa* 'Bonica') rises above the misty plumes of Mexican feather grass *(Nassella tenuissima)* in this Los Altos, California, garden designed by Richard McPherson. 'Bonica' is a delight at this time of year, and this rose's habit of producing scattered rebloom in summer and often another vibrant flush of flowers in fall makes it all the more appealing. Toward the end of the growing season, you'll begin to see the rose hips (small orange fruits) studding the canes. Likewise, the grass maintains its good looks through the season; its airy texture remains, but the silvery awns take on blonder tones as summer progresses. As an added bonus, Mexican feather grass holds its graceful form through winter, complementing the showy rose hips and providing interest even in the dark months of winter.

The lower-growing Mexican feather grass conceals the roses' relatively uninteresting stems. And the silky grass provides a soothing, neutral-colored space that distinguishes the bold rose blooms from the more-delicate but similarly-colored society garlic *(Tulbaghia violacea)* at the border edge.

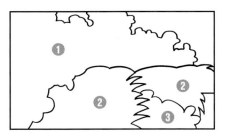

1. *Rosa* 'Bonica', 'Bonica' rose
2. *Nassella tenuissima,* Mexican feather grass
3. *Tulbaghia violacea,* society garlic

Eye-Catching Accents

If your goal is drama, a single clump of a carefully chosen ornamental grass is the ideal focal point for a front yard, the end of a path, or the corner of a deck or patio. With such a varied range of heights, growth habits, and colors to choose from, you are sure to find just the right one for your taste and needs.

At 4 to 6 feet tall, giant feather grass *(Stipa gigantea)* makes an excellent focal point, especially when placed in a sunny spot where light and breezes animate its beauty.

Most often, height is the main consideration when selecting a specimen grass, but you may also want to consider selections with showy variegated leaves, such as 'Cosmopolitan' miscanthus (*Miscanthus sinensis* var. *condensatus* 'Cosmopolitan'), which always draws the eye when planted in isolation. Bright golden grasses, and those with black, brown, or other unusual colors, also make compelling accents. Form, too, can elevate a grass to specimen status: consider the dramatic vertical effect of feather reed grass (*Calamagrostis* x *acutiflora*) or the spiky, symmetrical mounds of blue oat grass (*Helictotrichon sempervirens*).

Practically speaking, specimen plantings are a perfect way to enjoy large, clumping grasses, such as miscanthus and pampas grass, because they don't need dividing every few years. They can increase in girth without competing with companions for light, food, and space.

If a single clump of grass makes a striking accent, then imagine how impressive a mass planting can look. In this case, height usually isn't the primary consideration; after all, not too many home landscapes are large enough to support multiple clumps of big, bulky plants such as pampas grass (*Cortaderia selloana*). But ornamental grasses with distinctive forms, showy flowers, and colorful foliage all make excellent candidates for massing, even in smaller yards.

A mass can be as few as three plants or as many as you have room for. If you're working with spreading grasses rather than clumpers, just a few sprigs can eventually cover quite a bit of ground. Fortunately, it's easier to maintain spreading grasses as masses than as border plants. Simply mow around them regularly to control their spread, or plant them in a confined area, such as a strip of ground between a building and walkway, and you don't have to worry about their crowding out less vigorous bed and border companions.

For both specimen plants and mass plantings in a lawn area, use a metal or plastic edging strip to bar the turf grass from creeping or seeding into the ornamental grass. The edging not only keeps lawn grass out of the planting, but also keeps ornamental grasses, especially the creeping types, where you want them.

Colorful furniture and a ceramic pot combine with the bold pampas grass known as toe toe *(Cortaderia richardii)* to create a lively, inviting setting. (Garden of Linda Cochran, Bainbridge Island, Wash.)

Elegia capensis

Carex muskingumensis 'Oehme'

Stipa gigantea

ACCENT PLANTS

Carex muskingumensis 'Oehme'
'Oehme' palm sedge

Slow-spreading, 2-foot-tall clumps of somewhat sprawling stems clad in narrow, medium green leaves that develop yellow margins as the season goes on, turning all yellow to brown after the first hard frost; yellow-green flowers appear atop the stems in early summer. Sun (if soil is moist) to partial shade; average to evenly moist, humus-rich soil. *Zones 4 to 9*

Cortaderia selloana
Pampas grass

Broad clumps of green to gray-green leaves, evergreen in mild areas but tan in winter in cooler regions; huge, feathery, silvery white, cream, or pinkish plumes well above foliage on 8- to 12-foot-tall stalks in late summer to early fall, lasting into winter. Full sun; thrives in moist, fertile soil (shorter and slower growing if dry). *Zone 7 to 10*

Elegia capensis
Elegia

Dense clumps of 6- to 7-foot-tall cylindrical green stems accented with tufts of threadlike branches and papery pinkish brown-and-cream bracts at the stem joints. Outstanding as a specimen or in a large container. Full sun; evenly moist soil. *Zones 8 to 10*

Fargesia nitida
Fountain bamboo

Eight- to 14-foot-tall clumps of evergreen, upright, slender, deep purple and green or gray-green canes. Full sun or partial shade; average to moist, well-drained soil. *Zones 4 to 9*

Panicum virgatum 'Heavy Metal'
'Heavy Metal' switch grass

Three- to 4-foot-tall clumps of upright, blue-green leaves that turn bright yellow in fall, then tan in winter; mid- to late summer flowers are airy, pinkish to silvery panicles atop 4- to 5-foot-tall stems, lasting into winter. Full sun to light shade; adaptable, tolerates dry to wet soil. *Zones 5 to 9*

Stipa gigantea
Giant feather grass

Handsome, 2- to 3-foot tall clumps of upright to arching, narrow, grayish green leaves that are evergreen in mild climates. Open, golden flower panicles wave well above the foliage atop 5- to 7-foot-tall stems, starting in late spring or early summer and lasting into fall. Full sun; well-drained, fertile soil; tolerates coastal gardens and windy sites. *Zones 7 to 9*

A California Native

With its dynamic verticality, deer grass *(Muhlenbergia rigens)* enlivens any garden, refusing to be overlooked. Its dramatic shape and striking texture make it a superb choice for drawing attention to a special garden nook, as here at Strybing Arboretum, San Francisco.

Growing grasses as specimens allows you to capitalize on their true form and to site them for stunning visual effects. Free of companions, a specimen grass receives light from all angles, including the low-angled light of sunrise and sunset, which dramatically silhouettes the intricate form and details of even the most common grass. Observe how the sunlight bathes each fine stem of this deer grass, turning an already-handsome clump into a mass of silvery quills that are simply breath-taking against the darker background.

Deer grass is normally hardy only in Zones 7 and south, so if you want to re-create this effect in a cooler area, consider using blue oat grass *(Helictotrichon sempervirens)* as a substitute; it's hardy to Zone 4.

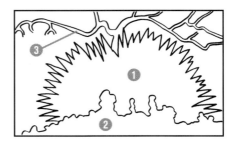

1. *Muhlenbergia rigens,* deer grass
2. *Zauschneria californica,* California fuchsia
3. *Aesculus californica,* California buckeye

SMALL IS BEAUTIFUL

Not surprisingly, some of the best-known ornamental grasses are quite large. It's hard to overlook a shrub-sized clump of maiden grass *(Miscanthus sinensis)* or the huge, showy plumes of pampas grass *(Cortaderia selloana)*. But many wonderful grasses are diminutive in comparison, perfect accents for even the tiniest spaces.

At only 4 to 6 inches high, buffalo grass *(Buchloe dactyloides)* makes a sturdy, drought-tolerant ground cover where its creeping roots can be confined by a barrier.

Look around your garden, and you're bound to discover lots of places that could benefit from low-growing grasses. Compact grasses make attractive edgings for beds and borders, as well as for lining paths, sidewalks, and other paved areas. You might consider removing a few bricks or pavers from your patio and using the holes as planting pockets for compact grass species and cultivars. These dainty miniatures are delightful when planted between stepping-stones, too.

The scaled-down size of compact grasses makes them ideal candidates for container plantings, either alone or mixed with colorful annuals and perennials. If you'd like a bit of green space but don't want to bother with weekly mowing, you can even make a pseudo-lawn out of low-growing grasses or sedges. (See Covering the Ground on page 118.)

When you plan and plant small gardens, part of the fun is choosing quality over quantity. Forget the old rule about planting in groups of three or more; when space is at a premium, it's far more rewarding to grow six different grasses than to have six that are identical.

Small gardens are a perfect opportunity for enjoying ornamental grasses having intricate flowers or fine-textured or delicately colored foliage, since the limited space invites close inspection of individual plants. Keep in mind, too, that each plant in a small garden should earn its keep, because there's no room to add fillers to take up the slack when featured plants don't look their best. Compact grasses with multiseason interest can be ideal when you want to spice up small spaces from spring to frost and beyond.

Having a small garden also affords you more time to give plants individual attention, so it's easier to keep a watchful eye on invasive grasses that might "get away" from you without regular intervention. You'll quickly spot (and can dig out) any runners that pop up where they're not wanted, and you can pull out unwanted self-sown seedlings as soon as they appear.

When you start searching for small-scale grasses, you'll find there are lots from which to choose. Some species are naturally low growing, while others are compact selections of normally tall-growing grasses. The words *dwarf, compact* or *compactum,* or *pumila* sometimes — but not always — appear in the names of these cultivars, as in *Phalaris arundinacea* 'Dwarf Garters' (commonly called

dwarf gardener's garters or dwarf ribbon grass). Variegated grasses — those with more than one color in their leaves — are often less vigorous than their solid-color cousins, making them practical choices for small spaces.

Keep in mind that cultivars chosen for compact size aren't suitable for every small space; dwarf pampas grass (*Corta-*

deria selloana 'Pumila'), for instance, can reach 6 feet tall in bloom, but that's considerably shorter than the average 8 to 12 feet of the species. If you're attracted to the overall effect of a normally tall grass but simply don't have room in your yard for a full-sized plant, one of these "compact" cultivars might be just what you need.

With a garden urn as an accent, this garden in miniature features 'Bronze' New Zealand hair sedge (*Carex comans* 'Bronze') and blue oat grass *(Helictotrichon sempervirens),* accompanied by a chartreuse-leaved *Spirea* 'Limemound'.

Molinia caerulea 'Variegata'

Carex conica 'Snowline'

Pennisetum alopecuroides 'Little Bunny'

SMALL SPACES

Acorus gramineus 'Pusillus'
Dwarf Japanese sweet flag
Slow-spreading, 3- to 5-inch-tall, ever-green carpets of dark green, fragrant foliage; inconspicuous flowers. Full sun to light shade; prefers evenly moist soil. *Zones 6 to 10*

Carex conica 'Snowline'
'Snowline' sedge
Slow-growing, 6- to 12-inch-tall clumps of narrow, deep green leaves edged in bright white; evergreen in mild climates; incon-spicuous flowers in late spring. Light shade; evenly moist, well-drained soil. *Zones 5 to 9*

Molinia caerulea 'Variegata'
Variegated purple moor grass
Tufted, 12- to 18-inch-tall clumps of green leaves with soft yellow vertical stripes; in fall, the leaves turn all yellow, then tan. Flowers are narrow, purple-tinted green panicles on slender 24- to 30-inch-tall stalks in midsummer, turning golden or tan and lasting into fall. Full sun (light shade in hot climates); moist, well-drained, fertile soil. *Zones 5 to 9*

Ophiopogon japonicus 'Nana'
Dwarf mondo grass
Spreading, evergreen carpets of short, leathery, dark green leaves that are about 4 inches tall; clusters of white flowers hidden among the leaves in early to midsummer. Partial shade; fertile, well-drained soil. *Zones 6 to 10*

Pennisetum alopecuroides 'Little Bunny'
'Little Bunny' fountain grass
Spiky, 10- to 12-inch-tall clumps of green leaves; short, fluffy, spikelike clusters of pinkish cream flowers atop 14- to 18-inch stems in late summer. Full sun to light shade; best in evenly moist but well-drained soil. *Zones 6 to 9*

A CITY SPACE

With a palette of soft foliage and flower colors, this wonderland of form and texture brings a sense of serenity to a surprisingly small space in this Seattle garden designed by Keith Geller. Bold and bright blooms, on the other hand, would have clamored for attention, making the space seem smaller and more confining. By selecting a few different plants and repeating them, it's possible to create informal drifts that invite the eye to travel over them and back again. The flowing masses of blue star creeper *(Pratia pedunculata)* combined with the sedges *(Carex albula* and *C. comans)* and blue oat grass *(Helictotrichon sempervirens)* create a miniature meadow. Imagine the same plants set out in discrete clumps: they'd be static and unmoving, not nearly so appealing. The tiny water feature also is a welcome addition to this small space, bringing a bit of the sky to earth and making an ideal mirror for the surrounding grasses.

As beautiful as this small-space planting is, it requires just minimal upkeep and will keep its inviting good looks throughout the season.

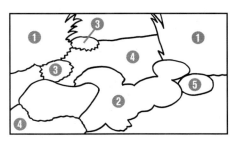

1. *Helictotrichon sempervirens,* blue oat grass
2. *Carex albula,* frosty curls sedge
3. *Carex comans,* New Zealand hair sedge
4. *Pratia pedunculata,* blue star creeper
5. *Lithodora diffusa,* lithospermum

By the Waterside

Ornamental grasses make perfect companions for traditional flowering water-garden favorites, such as water lily and lotus. Whether you have a large earth-lined pond or a small, plastic-lined, water-filled planter on your patio, grasses can bring height, color, texture, movement — even sound — to the scene.

Bowles' golden sedge (*Carex elata* 'Aurea') is a joyful presence in this small, backyard pond.

One of the most challenging aspects of planting a water garden can be how to deal with the edge, where the water meets the land (or the liner). Because a pond or water garden is typically set in or on a flat, open area, and still water naturally creates a strong horizontal view for the eye, plants that add vertical interest along the border are definitely welcome. Spiky, upright clumpers, such as common rush *(Juncus effusus)*, tend to give the garden edge a formal look, while fountainlike grasses lend a softer, more natural feel.

A single clump of grass can create a striking accent, but it can also play a dramatic role in a carefully orchestrated combination. Many moisture-loving plants have bold, broad leaves that contrast handsomely with slender grass foliage. Choose a grass cultivar that has bright yellow or variegated foliage, such as Bowles' golden sedge (*Carex elata* 'Aurea'), and you won't even need flowers: the grasses will provide color and textural contrast that you'll enjoy all season long.

Perhaps the most compelling reason to plant grasses near water is the potential for creating captivating reflections on the water's surface. In the proper light, water produces breathtaking mirrorlike effects, doubling the appeal of fluffy flower clusters and gently swaying foliage — something you and your garden visitors won't soon forget.

Grasses are amazingly versatile, so it's no surprise that many can adapt well to life in and around water gardens. Many of those described as appreciating evenly moist soil can tolerate or even thrive having several inches of standing water over their crowns, so you can actually plant them (or set their pots) inside the water's edge.

For planting around a water garden, your options are practically unlimited. The bank of an earth-lined pond acts somewhat like a raised bed — the plant's crown is not soggy, but the roots have access to a generous supply of moisture — providing ideal growing conditions for a wide range of grasses. And if you're planting around a water feature within a man-made liner, the surrounding soil won't be any different than the soil in the rest of your garden, so whatever you can grow in other parts of your yard should grow well there.

Grasses growing with ample moisture tend to be quite vigorous, so you'll probably need to divide and replant them every few years (or even every year, if they are growing in pots). Early spring is generally the best time to do this, so the plants have plenty of time to get new roots established before cold weather returns.

For water-garden grasses grown in containers, a standard plastic nursery pot will work fine. (The pot needn't be anything special to look at, since it will be hidden from view under the water's surface.) Before planting the grass, line the pot with some natural burlap to keep the soil from sifting out of the drainage holes in the pot's base. Fill the pot with good, heavy garden soil — the best thing for submerged plants — then plant the grass. Firm the soil around the roots, then spread an inch or two of gravel over the top of the pot.

Most marginal grasses grow well with 2 to 4 inches of water over their crowns, though cattail (*Typha* spp.) and some other taller grasses can tolerate deeper water. If you designed your pond with stepped sides, or if you used a rigid liner with built-in ledges, you may need to set one or several bricks (or a cinder block or two) under the pots to bring them up to the proper level relative to the surface of the water. (Plastic milk crates work well, too, if you need more height.)

Water-garden grasses should do just fine without supplemental feeding, especially if you repot them in fresh soil each year. If you do choose to fertilize, look for

a low-nitrogen product; otherwise, the extra nitrogen in the water will encourage algae growth. In fall, before the first frost, remove tender grasses from the garden and bring them, pot and all, indoors for the winter. Hardy grasses need little attention; simply cut back the declining dormant top growth above the water level so it doesn't fall into the water and rot.

Marginals, such as common rush *(Juncus effusus)* and scouring rush *(Equisetum hyemale),* make a man-made garden pond appear more natural.

Juncus effusus 'Unicorn'

Typha latifolia 'Variegata'

Equisetum hyemale

WATER GARDENS

Equisetum hyemale
Scouring rush, horsetail
Vigorously spreading, 2- to 6-foot-tall clumps of cylindrical, gray-green to bright green stems with cream-colored bands accented by black fringe; stems bronze-green in winter; flowers are conelike spikes at the stem tips. Full sun to partial shade; adaptable but thrives in evenly moist, fertile soil or up to 4 inches of standing water. *Zones 5 to 10*

Glyceria maxima 'Variegata'
Variegated manna grass
Fast-spreading, 24- to 30-inch-tall masses of upright to arching, green leaves with broad, butter yellow vertical stripes, tinted with pink in spring and fall; may produce loose, brownish flower panicles in mid- to late summer. Full sun; best in moist soil or up to 8 inches of standing water. *Zones 5 to 10*

Juncus effusus 'Unicorn'
Corkscrew rush
Loose 1- to 2-foot-tall clumps of curiously curled and twisted, medium to dark green stems; clusters of yellowish to brown flowers appear in early summer. Full sun to light shade; evenly moist to wet soil. *Zones 6 to 9*

Schoenoplectus lacustris
  ssp. *tabernaemontani* 'Zebrinus'
Zebra rush, banded bulrush
Moderate spreader with 2- to 4-foot-tall, upright, leafless, cylindrical, dark green stems having horizontal, light yellow stripes; clusters of brownish flowers appear in midsummer and last into winter. Full sun (light shade in hot climates); evenly moist soil or up to about 6 inches of standing water. *Zones 5 to 9*

Typha latifolia 'Variegata'
Variegated cattail
Moderately spreading clumps of upright, gray-green, white-striped leaves that turn golden yellow in fall; mid- to late-summer flowers atop 4- to 6-foot-tall stems are long, brown, cigar-shaped inflorescences with male flowers on the top and females below, turning deep brown and lasting into winter. Full sun; evenly moist, fertile soil or up to about 12 inches of standing water. *Zones 4 to 9*

A SOOTHING WATER GARDEN

All too frequently, it seems, ambitious homeowners expend considerable effort to install their dream water garden only to find themselves disappointed by the results. The water lilies may be beautiful, but the garden itself looks artificial and out of place. The answer? Use grasses to soften a harsh transition between the water and the lawns beyond, as well as add some much needed vertical interest.

A single grass makes an elegant formal accent, whereas a mixture of grasses with different heights and habits — such as these at Heronswood Nursery, Kingston, Washington — creates a more private, nat-ural-looking space. Those with colorful foliage, such as the golden wood millet (*Milium effusum* 'Aureum'), Bowles' golden sedge (*Carex elata* 'Aurea'), and New Zealand hair sedge (*Carex comans*) used in this design, are especially adept at livening up the scene.

When choosing grasses to complement a water feature, you'll probably find that plants that naturally grow near water are most appropriate. But if your pond has an artificial liner, amend the soil with a gener-ous supply of organic matter to help it hold moisture, as it won't be any wetter than the soil in the other parts of your garden.

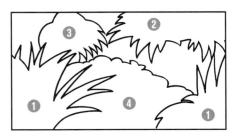

1. *Milium effusum* 'Aureum', golden wood millet
2. *Carex elata* 'Aurea', Bowles' golden sedge
3. *Carex comans,* New Zealand hair sedge
4. *Nymphaea* sp., water lily

Aglow with Autumn Color

Many gardeners think that grasses don't truly come into their own until they don their showy end-of-season hues. Ornamental grasses offer countless opportunities for autumn excitement, many having fall foliage that will set your landscape ablaze with color. Some grasses hold their color well into winter.

The characteristic pendulous flowers of wild oats *(Chasmanthium latifolium)* turn copper-red in fall, often remaining into winter, weathered to a light gray-green.

Autumn is the time of year when warm-season grasses truly surprise and delight. They've had all summer to soak up the sun, so by fall they've reached their full height and are ready to share a showy display. Those that haven't yet begun to bloom now send up their flowers in a race to ripen their seeds before cold weather returns; others keep up their summer bloom display well into autumn. Some even rival deciduous shrubs and trees for glorious fall color, from candy-apple red and copper-penny pink to glowing orange and sunshine yellow.

The lower temperatures of autumn can also bring out color changes in a few cool-season grasses. Purple moor grass *(Molinia caerulea),* for example, turns an arresting golden yellow. And some variegated grasses, such as 'Northern Lights' tufted hair grass *(Deschampsia cespitosa* 'Northern Lights') and Feesey's gardener's garters *(Phalaris arundinacea* 'Feesey'), add a pinkish cast to their yellow- or white-striped leaves.

Evergreen shrubs make handsome backdrops for bright-hued grass foliage, with many deciduous shrubs contributing red, orange, pink, purple, and yellow shades to the spectacular parade of color.

Fall-flowering annuals and perennials add an extra level of interest, in a veritable rainbow of hues, to either contrast with or complement ornamental grasses. The jewel tones of rich purple New England asters *(Aster novae-angliae)* and deep blue monkshoods *(Aconitum* spp.), for instance, positively glow against the lemon yellow or coppery fall foliage of many miscanthus. With so many lovely late-blooming flowers from which to choose, exciting color companions for your glorious grasses are almost unlimited.

For grasses that turn color in fall, full sun generally brings out the most brilliant color changes. Those growing in light shade will change color, too, but the hues will be more muted.

Remember that a grass with exceptional fall color in one area or climate may show little or no interesting color change in another region. Even in the same garden, the intensity of the display can vary from year to year, depending on the weather conditions. To get a general idea of what a particular grass can offer, plan fall visits to botanical gardens and to garden-center plantings in your area that feature grasses.

The flower heads of *Miscanthus sinensis* 'Positano' are the centerpiece of this stunning garden aglow with other fall favorites such as Russian sage *(Perovskia atriplicifolia)* and *Sedum* 'Autumn Joy'.

Molinia caerulea ssp. *arundinacea* 'Skyracer'

Miscanthus sinensis 'November Sunset'

Panicum virgatum

FALL COLOR

Andropogon spp.
Andropogons
Clump-forming, warm-season grasses prized for their orange, coppery, or reddish purple fall colors; height varies by species. Full sun; adapted to a wide range of soil conditions. *Zones 3, 4, 5, or 6 to 10, depending on the species*

Anemanthele lessoniana
Pheasant's-tail grass
Also known as *Stipa arundinacea;* dense 2- to 3-foot-tall clumps of arching, medium green leaves with rusty tints that are particularly noticeable from late summer through winter; arching, reddish flower panicles just above the leaves in summer. Full sun (for best color) to light shade; average, well-drained soil. *Zones 8 to 10*

Miscanthus sinensis
Japanese silver grass
Four- to 6-foot-tall clumps of upright to arching green leaves that turn yellow, purplish, or reddish orange in fall; branched flower clusters appear above the leaves in late summer and fall. 'November Sunset' is a particularly late-blooming selection. *Miscanthus* 'Purpurascens' has exceptional fall foliage color. Full sun; average to evenly moist, well-drained soil. *Zones 5 or 6 to 9*

Molinia caerulea ssp. *arundinacea*
Purple moor grass
Tufted, 1- to 2-foot-tall clumps of green to bluish green leaves that turn golden yellow in fall, then reddish brown, then tan. 'Skyracer' has particularly tall flower stems (8 to 9 feet in bloom). Full sun (light shade in hot climates); evenly moist but well-drained, fertile soil. *Zones 4 to 9*

Panicum virgatum
Switch grass
Clump-forming to moderately spreading, 3- to 6-foot-tall clumps of mostly upright leaves that are green to gray-green, usually turning yellow in fall but can also be reddish, orange, or purplish. 'Shenandoah' starts taking on reddish tints as early as midsummer, turning purplish red in fall. Leaves are 3 to 6 feet tall; flowers are 4 to 8 feet tall. Full sun to light shade; tolerates dry to wet soil. *Zones 4 or 5 to 9*

Spodiopogon sibiricus
Frost grass
Handsome, upright, 2- to 3-foot-tall clumps of hairy, nearly horizontal, bright green leaves that take on purplish red color in fall, then turn tan after frost. Full sun to partial shade; evenly moist but well-drained, fertile soil. *Zones 5 to 9*

A Rich Harvest

Cooler-climate gardeners may not be able to enjoy the colorful foliage of tender grasses year-round, but they get something just as good — a tremendous display of striking fall color from many warm-season grasses. Switch grasses, such as *Panicum virgatum* 'Heavy Metal' shown in this Orinda, California, garden design by Suzanne Porter, are an excellent choice for dependable fall interest. This selection usually changes to yellow and orange hues; other switch grass cultivars, such as 'Hänse Herms' and 'Shenandoah', tend to a deeper maroon.

The harvest hues of warm-season grasses make excellent complements for the richly-colored blooms of fall-flowering asters. In this garden, the orange grass makes an outstanding backdrop for the deep purple-blue aster 'Climax' *(Aster novae-angliae* 'Climax').

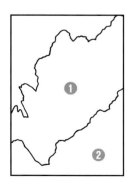

1. *Panicum virgatum* 'Heavy Metal', 'Heavy Metal' switch grass
2. *Aster novae-angliae* 'Climax', New England aster

PROBLEM-SOLVERS

ABOVE: This impressive gold-variegated miscanthus (*Miscanthus sinensis* 'Goldfeder'), like the similar 'Silberfeder', would make an excellent privacy screen.

OPPOSITE: A perfect example of right plants, right place. Prairie dropseed *(Sporobolus heterolepis)* and Russian sage *(Perovskia atriplicifolia)* create drifts of refreshing color in this dry-soil garden.

Ornamental grasses offer more than just pretty foliage and flowers: they're practical problem-solvers, too. These sturdy, adaptable plants give resourceful gardeners a viable option for bringing beauty to less-than-ideal sites.

Of course, not all grasses are equally well suited for all conditions. As with any plant, it's important first to identify what the conditions are, then to find out which grasses are best able to cope with that challenge. Sometimes, the perfect grass for a difficult site is one that you'd never turn loose in the ideal growing conditions of your well-tended beds and borders. Species with wide-spreading roots, for instance, can quickly run rampant and crowd out less aggressive companions in loose, rich soil. But their spreading root systems make these same grasses the ideal choice for planting on a slope, because they provide quick cover and discourage erosion.

Grasses also have much to offer a gardener faced with a difficult landscaping problem, such as a narrow, hard-to-mow strip between sidewalk and street. The graceful, flowing foliage of grasses makes them ideal for softening hard edges along pathways and buildings. Farther away from the house, taller grass can serve as effective, fast-growing screens, giving you privacy without the expense of a fence or a hedge. And if you're searching for a great-looking ground cover that's less work than the usual lawn grass, any number of ornamental grasses provide colorful, imaginative results. Whatever your landscape problem, with a bit of research and creativity you can find an ornamental grass that meets the challenge.

Celebrating Hot, Dry Sites

Heat- and drought-tolerant, many ornamental grasses are a natural choice for sun-baked sites and parched planting strips that border buildings and sidewalks — difficult spots that can pose a major maintenance problem. These tough plants are also an excellent choice in climates where rainfall is scarce, or at least undependable.

FIRE-SMART GRASS GARDENING

Dry-climate gardeners have more than a lack of rain to deal with — the threat of wildfires can be a serious problem, too. If you live where fires are a seasonal hazard, think long and hard about how you wish to use ornamental grasses in your landscape *before* you plant them. Because of the quantity of dry stalks and leaves on tall grasses, flying sparks and embers can ignite an entire planting, possibly leading the fire right to your door.

For this reason, always err on the side of caution. In dry climates, keep plantings of ornamental grasses at least 50 feet — and ideally farther — from the walls of your home. If you insist on having grasses closer to your home than this, choose low-growing species. Lush, green leaves are slower to ignite than dry foliage, so consider irrigating your grasses regularly to keep them from becoming tinder. Cut down any grasses that go dormant, especially during fire season, and remove the dry debris to eliminate possible fuel sources.

When you're choosing grasses for dry sites, it's natural to seek out species that are characterized as "drought tolerant." But in reality, the ability of any plant to tolerate drought depends on how the term *drought* is defined and the context in which it is used. In a climate that regularly receives an inch of rainfall per week during the growing season, a rainless period as brief as three weeks could be considered a drought. In areas where plants are accustomed to drier conditions, it may take four to six weeks, or even longer, for them to show signs of drought stress.

Another factor to consider is how much watering you are willing and able to do. If the grasses must survive on rainfall only with no supplemental irrigation, choose grasses that are known to be drought tolerant. But if you can water at least once every two or three weeks when it fails to rain, many more plant options are available. If you water early in the season, you must keep at it, because your grasses will become accustomed to having plenty of moisture close to the soil surface. If your area routinely experiences mid- and late summer dry spells, omit early-summer irrigation to encourage your plants to develop deeper root systems and toughen up a little.

Requiring a plant to tolerate dry soil generally results in shorter stems, reduced spread, and a less lush overall effect than the same plant would have with ample moisture. Still, that's not necessarily a bad thing. For instance, because of their stunted size and spread, grasses growing in hot, dry sites will seldom, if ever, need to be staked. And creeping grasses that quickly romp through moist-soil sites will be noticeably constrained in drier sites, allowing you to enjoy their beauty without worrying that they'll take over the garden.

In exceptionally dry conditions, you may have the most success growing cool-season grasses, such as blue fescue *(Festuca glauca)*. These species grow most actively in fall, winter, and spring, when temperatures are moderate and moisture is more abundant. They go dormant in

summer, making do with only a fraction of the moisture required by actively growing warm-season grasses. Cool-season grasses generally don't have the lush look you expect from summer plantings; their foliage may be partially or even totally brown, or perhaps just dull and off-color. But if you combine them with drought-tolerant annuals and perennials, the grasses can rest quietly during the hottest part of summer, returning to grace your garden with exuberant foliage during the cooler months.

From a color standpoint, green- and blue-leaved grasses are best in hot, dry sites. Strong sun and dry soil tends to be unforgiving on grasses with golden foliage, bleaching or burning it. Grasses with bold variegation, such as some of the *Miscanthus* cultivars, can also get a little crisp in hot, dry, sunny areas.

RIGHT: *Festuca glauca* 'Elijah Blue' is one of the best of the blue fescues. It pairs well with the silvery soft foliage of lamb's ears *(Stachys byzantina)*.

LEFT: The restio *Chondropetalum tectorum* joins in a drought-loving grouping with a blue-leaved sedum *(Sedum spathulifolium* 'Cape Blanco') and maroon-leaved *Geranium* 'Midnight Reiter'. (Garden of Linda Cochran, Bainbridge Island, Wash.)

Lots of sun? That's no problem for the vast majority of ornamental grasses. But while most grasses can get by with less water than the average garden perennial, they still require some water to survive. Fortunately, the helpful hints that follow can drastically reduce the amount of water you'll need to supply for good growth.

First, make sure that any rainfall you receive gets into the soil and *stays* there until the plant's roots are able to reach it. Consider lowering the surface of the planting area an inch or two below the surrounding ground level to help catch and hold the water until it can soak in. This approach is particularly useful in planting areas bordered by paving; otherwise, water running off the paving will rush by instead of soaking into the ground, washing away some soil in the process.

In sandy and clay conditions, work ample amounts of organic matter into the soil to improve moisture retention. But keep in mind that this isn't a permanent solution: no matter how thoroughly you amend the soil before planting, even the toughest organic matter will break down after a few years in hot, dry conditions. Each time you dig and divide the grasses, therefore, remember to add compost or other organic material to the hole before you replant, to help keep up the humus levels. And always mulch generously. Mulches encourage water to soak into the soil, especially heavy clay, by keeping the surface from hardening and crusting over.

Finally, recall that even drought-tolerant grasses will need some supplemental watering during their first year — and perhaps even the second — if rainfall is lacking. Once established, the extensive root system of the grasses will be able to seek out water deep in the soil; when just planted, however, the immature root system must make do with whatever moisture is close by. Giving your new hot-and-dry-site plantings a little extra attention during the first season will definitely pay off later in healthy growth and water savings.

Blue oat grass *(Helictotrichon sempervirens)* forms a dependable ground cover on a dry slope. *Phormium* 'Dark Delight' provides color contrast and a strong anchor at the base of the steps.

HOT, DRY SITES

Achnatherum hymenoides
Indian rice grass

Also known as *Oryzopsis hymenoides*; clumps of 12- to 18-inch tall, narrow leaves are bright green in spring and tan in summer, lasting into winter; airy, open flower panicles atop 2-foot-tall stems in early spring. Full sun; average, well-drained to dry soil. *Zones 5 (or colder with excellent drainage) to 10*

Bouteloua gracilis
Blue grama grass

Six- to 8-inch-tall clumps of narrow green leaves that take on purplish tints in fall, then turn tan for winter; flowers are silvery pink or purplish spikelets clustered into little combs at the tips of 12- to 18-inch-tall stems, starting in early summer and lasting for several months. Full sun; average, well-drained soil. *Zones 3 to 10*

Muhlenbergia capillaris
Pink muhly, purple muhly

Also known as *Muhlenbergia filipes*; 2-foot-tall clumps of glossy, deep green leaves; cloudlike panicles of purplish pink flowers atop 3- to 4-foot stems in early to late fall. Full sun to light shade; prefers moist, well-drained soil but is drought-tolerant. *Zones 7 to 9*

Schizachyrium scoparium
Little bluestem

Also known as *Andropogon scoparius*; 3- to 4-foot-tall clumps of mostly upright stems with green to bluish green leaves, turning orange to reddish brown in fall and holding some color into winter; late summer to fall flowers appear in small, silvery tufts near the stem tips. Full sun (tolerates light shade); good drought tolerance but best in evenly moist, well-drained soil. *Zones 3 to 9*

Sorghastrum nutans
Indian grass

Three- to 4-foot-tall clumps of mostly upright, green to blue-green leaves, turning yellow or orange in fall, then tan in winter; reddish tan flower panicles atop 5- to 6-foot-tall stems in late summer into fall, turning tan and lasting through most of winter. Full sun (tolerates light shade); tallest in moist soil, but drought-tolerant when established. *Zones 4 to 9*

Bouteloua gracilis

Schizachyrium scoparium

Sorghastrum nutans

A Colorful Dry Garden

Hot and dry sites should no longer be considered wastelands for gravel and cactus when a good number of grasses do well in these challenging spots, easily shrugging off drought and heat. This splendid garden at Korbel Winery, Forestville, California, is a superb example of how pairing appropriate grasses with compatible companion plants can transform even a troublesome site into a lovely landscape feature. The pink-and-white butterfly blooms of gaura *(Gaura lindheimeri)* make an artful bridge between the rosy purple coneflowers *(Echinacea purpurea)* behind and the fluffy white flower heads of feathertop *(Pennisetum villosum)* in front, punctuated by the ever-impressive towering giant feather grass *(Stipa gigantea)*.

Feathertop is a charming grass, but be aware that it can become a serious weed in areas where it's hardy (Zones 8 to 10). In cooler climates, though, you could enjoy it as an annual.

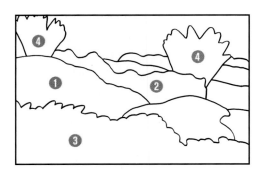

1. *Gaura lindheimeri,* gaura
2. *Echinacea purpurea,* purple coneflower
3. *Pennisetum villosum,* feathertop
4. *Stipa gigantea,* giant feather grass

The Luxury of Moist Soils

Although soggy sites can present a landscaping challenge, they also offer ideal conditions for vigorous plant growth. Fortunately, many outstanding ornamental grasses appreciate having "wet feet" for all or part of the year. Pair them with moisture-loving flowering and foliage perennials for an unforgettable garden.

Three moisture lovers — giant reed (*Arundo donax)*, variegated miscanthus (*Miscanthus sinensis* 'Variegatus'), and variegated prairie cord grass (*Spartina pectinata* 'Aureomarginata') — are set off by bright yellow daylilies (*Hemerocallis* sp.).

When grasses have access to a generous and dependable water supply, they can send up tall stems and put on lots of leafy growth. The same species that grow 3 to 4 feet tall in average garden soil can shoot up to 6 feet or more in height when the soil is moist. That puts them in perfect scale with tall-growing flowering perennials, such as tall coreopsis *(Coreopsis tripteris)*, Joe Pye weed *(Eupatorium maculatum)*, queen-of-the-prairie *(Filipendula venusta)*, and ironweed (*Vernonia* spp.). Both perennials and grasses benefit from having companions of similar stature. (Not only do single clumps of towering plants look out of place in a border scaled for the home garden, but generally they also require special staking or pruning to stay in proper proportion. When they're with like-sized companions, though, the plants simply lean on each other for support.)

Moist-soil sites also offer endless opportunities for enchanting foliage contrasts. Unlike dry-soil plants, which often have slender or deeply cut foliage to reduce water loss through the leaf surfaces, many soggy-soil perennials produce luxuriant masses of large, broad leaves. The slender, spiky, or arching foliage of grasses provides a striking contrast to the bold leaves of umbrella

plant *(Darmera peltata)*, ligularia (*Ligularia* spp.), and rodgersia (*Rodgersia* spp.), to name just a few large-leaved, moisture-loving perennials.

To give yourself even more ornamental grass options for wet spots, consider constructing raised beds. Elevating the soil surface just a few inches will keep the crowns of the grasses out of the mire, reducing the likelihood of rot. And a site with well-drained soil around the crowns and ample moisture in the root zone offers ideal conditions for a wide variety of grasses and perennials, allowing you to grow lush borders filled with flowers and foliage without having to provide much, if any, extra water.

To make a raised bed, work a generous amount of compost, chopped leaves, or other organic matter into the soil. Spread 2 to 4 inches of organic matter over the site, and dig or till it into the soil. The cultivation loosens and aerates the soil, and the bulk from the organic matter raises the surface of the finished bed several inches. Alternatively, you might choose to bring in good-quality topsoil and spread a layer several inches deep over the site. With this approach, you don't get the benefits of loosening the soil and adding organic matter, and it can get pricey if you have a large area to cover. Still, this method is usually quicker, and it may be the only option available to you if you're not willing or able to dig or till.

Not all moist-soil sites are created equal. The banks of ponds and streams tend to be moist most if not all of the time, depending on the water level. Low-lying sites, on the other hand, are often waterlogged in spring, when rainfall is more abundant. As the weather gets warmer and drier, however, the surface of saturated low-lying areas tends to dry out, though the ground beneath may remain relatively wet. Many moisture-loving grasses can do well in either situation, although they do appreciate supplemental watering during dry spells when moisture is lacking. If you're dealing with a spot that is wet primarily in spring, delay digging a new garden until late summer or fall when the soil will be drier and easier to work.

Elegantly simple and refreshingly cool, white Peter Pan Series zinnias and 'Sun and Shade' impatiens settle comfortably at the foot of a large clump of variegated miscanthus (*Miscanthus sinensis* 'Variegatus').

Juncus effusus 'Carman's Japanese'

Phalaris arundinacea 'Picta'

Spartina pectinata 'Aureomarginata'

MOISTURE-LOVERS

Acorus calamus
Sweet flag

Moderately spreading clumps of relatively broad, fragrant, green, irislike foliage; greenish yellow flower spikes in late spring to early summer on 3- to 4-foot-tall stems. 'Variegatus' has green leaves with creamy yellow vertical stripes. Full sun (light shade in hot climates); evenly moist soil to several inches of standing water. *Zones 4 to 10*

Carex grayi
Gray's sedge

Two- to 3-foot-tall clumps of light to medium green leaves that hold their color well into fall or early winter; early to mid-summer flowers are large, rounded, yellow-green "maces" with distinct spikes, drying to brown. Partial shade; moist soil to shallow water in spring (somewhat drier conditions okay in summer). *Zones 4 to 9*

Eriophorum angustifolium
Cotton grass

Spreading, 18-inch-tall clumps of light green leaves; flowers are fluffy white tufts atop 2-foot-tall stems in spring, lasting for months. Full sun; moist to wet soil. *Zones 4 to 8*

Juncus effusus 'Carman's Japanese'
'Carman's Japanese' rush

Also known as *Juncus carmens;* clumps of slender, bright green, evergreen stems usually 2 to 3 feet tall; cream-colored flowers followed by reddish brown seed heads in summer. Full sun to light shade; evenly moist soil to several inches of standing water. *Zones 4 to 10*

Phalaris arundinacea 'Picta'
Gardener's garters

Spreading, 2- to 3-foot-tall masses of upright green leaves with vertical white stripes. Full sun to partial shade; adaptable but prefers evenly moist, fertile soil. *Zones 4 to 9*

Spartina pectinata 'Aureomarginata'
Variegated prairie cord grass

Fast-spreading, 4-to 5-foot-tall plants with arching, long, narrow, glossy green leaves with thin yellow margins, turning all yellow in fall, then tan; flowers are yellowish brown panicles on 6-foot-tall stems in late summer and early fall; not especially showy. Full sun to light shade; prefers evenly moist, well-drained soil but adapts. *Zone 3 to 9*

LUSH AND LIVELY

Quite a few grasses can adapt to evenly moist soil, but it takes a special grass to make a strong show in a site that's soggy *and* shady. Golden Hakone grass (*Hakonechloa macra* 'Aureola') is a true gem, illuminating even the darkest corner with its graceful, golden, bamboolike foliage. It tolerates dry conditions, but with generous moisture it spreads steadily into elegant, arching mounds.

Dramatic solo, golden Hakone grass looks even better with well-chosen companions. In this Napa, California, garden designed by Freeland Tanner, golden creeping Jenny (*Lysimachia nummularia*

'Aurea') creates a ground-hugging carpet of chartreuse, penny-sized leaves, making a striking contrast to the slender blades of Hakone grass. Equally effective, hostas' broad, textured foliage and bold, mounded forms provide another foil for the finer-leaved grass.

All of these plants can tolerate considerable sun as long as the soil doesn't dry out, so feel free to plant them in and out of the shade. For similar textures but a different color balance, the all-green species form of Hakone grass is a subtler but still lovely alternative to the golden-leaved cultivar.

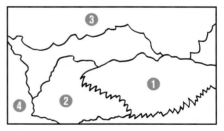

1. *Hakonechloa macra* 'Aureola', golden Hakone grass

2. *Lysimachia nummularia* 'Aurea', golden creeping Jenny

3. *Hosta* sp., hosta

4. *Rosa* sp., rose

Made for the Shade

Most ornamental grasses thrive in sun, but if you choose your plants well, you can enjoy their beauty even if your garden is a bit on the shady side. Several grasses and grasslike plants positively thrive with shade, often gaining their best color with less light, and many more can tolerate fewer hours of full sun.

Graceful frosty curls sedge *(Carex albula)* makes a nice textural contrast with *Heuchera* and *Hostas,* edging a shady gravel path.
(Elisabeth C. Miller Botanical Garden, Seattle)

Generally speaking, a shade garden receives less than six hours of sun per day. It may sound like a cut-and-dried definition, but in reality *shade* is a relative term. There are as many kinds of shade as there are gardeners. You'll find dense, all-day, year-round shade under evergreen trees, and spring sun and summer shade under deciduous trees (this varies, too, depending on the tree).

One side of your house may get full morning sun and full afternoon shade, or vice versa — or even morning shade, full midday sun, and then full shade again in late afternoon. There's shade with evenly moist soil, and there's shade with bone-dry soil. Considering all this, it's not difficult to deduce that a plant adapted to one kind of shade may not do well in another "shady" spot.

Typically, you'll be most successful with grasses when you plant them in the brightest spot you can offer. Just an hour or two of direct sunlight can make the difference between a healthy, good-looking grass and a weakling that fades away after a few seasons. If you're gardening under deciduous trees, try cool-season grasses: they'll receive plenty of sun from late fall until early summer when the canopy returns, about the same time the grasses go dormant.

If you're dealing with heavier shade, such as that cast by a building or an evergreen tree, try grasslike plants, such as mondo grasses (*Ophiopogon* spp.), lilyturfs (*Liriope* spp.), and sedges (*Carex* spp.). These plants generally make do with much less light than true grasses, while still providing a range of foliage colors and textures, and delightful flowers and fruits.

Some grasses are at their best in the shade. Light shade tends to bring out the most vibrant colors in gold-leaved and variegated grasses, for instance. And grasses that prefer full sun in northern gardens appreciate some shelter from the hottest part of a sultry summer day in southern climates.

Shady spots also inspire dramatic plant combinations. Many shade-loving perennials produce large, lush leaves — think of hosta, heuchera (*Heuchera* spp.), and Lenten rose (*Helleborus* x *hybridus*), to name a few — which make striking foils for the slender blades of grasses and grasslike plants. The shade-welcoming golden and variegated grasses deftly illumine dark-leaved companions, such as Robb's wood spurge *(Euphorbia robbiae)* and bearsfoot hellebore (*Helleborus foetidus)*, whereas grasses with green leaves complement silvery lungwort (*Pulmonaria* hybrids), cream-marbled Italian arum (*Arum italicum* 'Pictum'), and the gray-and-maroon fronds of Japanese painted fern (*Athyrium goeringianum* 'Pictum').

Grasses in shady spots generally require less water than the same plants in a sunny site. That's a good thing, because shaded spots may be on the dry side when rainfall is lacking, particularly when extensive networks of tree roots compete with grasses and other perennials for water. Working plenty of organic matter into the soil at planting time, maintaining a layer of organic mulch over the soil, and watering with a soaker hose or drip irrigation system during dry spells will help ensure consistently great-looking grasses in your shade garden.

TROUBLE IN PARADISE

One word of warning: during the damp days of spring, slugs and snails can be a serious threat to all of your shade plants. They adore hostas and other lush leaves but can also damage tender, emerging grass foliage. Fortunately, most grasses are vigorous enough to outgrow these pests, but you still may be left with damaged leaf tips. If slugs and snails are a problem in your garden, try trapping them in shallow containers of grape juice or beer. Or set the rinds of your breakfast citrus or melons around the garden, then lift them daily and scrape the collected slugs and snails into a bucket of soapy water. Over time, you'll gradually notice a decline in numbers of these troublesome pests, and all of your shade plants will thank you.

Arrhenatherum elatius ssp. *bulbosum*
'Variegatum'

Chasmanthium latifolium

Milium effusum 'Aureum'

SHADE-LOVERS

Arrhenatherum elatius ssp. *bulbosum* 'Variegatum'
Variegated bulbous oat grass

Loose, 1-foot-tall clumps of narrow green leaves with white vertical stripes. Prefers cool temperatures; may go summer-dormant in hot, humid areas; cut back before flowering and water to encourage new fall growth. Full sun to partial shade; average to moist, fertile soil. *Zones 4 to 9*

Chasmanthium latifolium
Wild oats, northern sea oats

Also known as *Uniola latifolia;* upright, 2- to 3-foot-tall clumps of light green leaves that turn copper-brown in fall and stay brown in winter; open panicles of dangling, flat green to brown spikelets appear atop nodding, 3- to 4-foot-tall stems in late summer and last through most of winter. Best in partial shade; adaptable but prefers evenly moist, well-drained, rich soil. *Zones 5 to 9*

Deschampsia flexuosa
Crinkled hair grass

Dense, 1-foot-tall, evergreen clumps of shiny, fine-textured green foliage; airy panicles of glossy, yellow-brown or purple-tinted spikelets atop 2-foot-tall stems in midsummer. Partial shade (sun in cool climates); evenly moist, well-drained, humus-rich soil. *Zones 4 to 8*

Hystrix patula
Bottlebrush grass

One-foot-tall clumps of upright green leaves, tan in fall; 3- to 4-foot-tall stems with bottlebrush-like, green spikes in mid-summer, turning brown and shattering by fall. Partial shade; can tolerate dry soil but prefers moist but well-drained, fertile soil. *Zones 4 to 9*

Luzula nivea
Snowy woodrush

Slow-spreading, tufted, 1-foot-tall carpets of narrow, gray-green, hairy-edged leaves that are evergreen in mild climates; dense clusters of cottony white flowers atop 2-foot-tall stems in late spring to early summer, turning tan. Partial shade; adaptable but prefers evenly moist but well-drained, humus-rich soil. *Zone 4 to 9*

Milium effusum 'Aureum'
Golden wood millet

Clumps of 18-inch-tall leaves that are bright yellow in spring and light green by summer. Best for cool-season color, as plants go partly summer-dormant in hot conditions. Light shade; cool, moist, humus-rich soil. *Zones 6 to 9*

A Shade-Lover's Garden

Shady spots are perfect places to experiment with foliage color and texture. Bright green, blue, and golden grasses are obvious possibilities, but dark-leaved plants can also be quite effective. When using dark-leaved grasses, the key is to pair them with lighter companions, which add a hint of brightness and visual interest wherever they are placed. This simple but stunning combination featured at Elisabeth C. Miller Botanical Garden in Seattle takes this rule of thumb one step further: the companion plant has both light and dark elements. The pale green, feathery fronds of western maidenhair fern *(Adiantum aleuticum)* give the moody-hued black mondo grass *(Ophiopogon planiscapus* 'Nigrescens') a lift, and the fern's black stems artfully echo the dark, arching blades of mondo grass. Details such as this turn good-looking gardens into memorable showplaces.

If black mondo grass is a mite too Gothic for your tastes, then look to the sedges and other ferns for striking shade color and texture, any of which would make a handsome companion for a shade-tolerant grass or sedge.

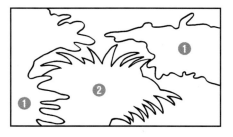

1. *Adiantum aleuticum,* western maidenhair fern
2. *Ophiopogon planiscapus* 'Nigrescens', black mondo grass

Coping with Slopes

Sloping sites offer gardeners a tough landscaping challenge: Left unplanted, slopes can erode over time; turf-covered, they resist erosion, but they pose major maintenance problems. Ornamental grasses, on the other hand, control erosion without the weekly maintenance chores, such as the dreaded mowing.

Dependable grasses like these can be put to work covering a problem slope: from front to back, giant feather grass *(Stipa gigantea)*, Mexican feather grass *(Nassella tenuissima)*, purple fountain grass *(Pennisetum setaceum* 'Rubrum'), and Japanese silver grass *(Miscanthus sinensis)*. *Phormium* and the dark purple shrub *Cotinus* provide strong accents.

What makes grasses such a good choice for slopes? Their extensive root systems. The fibrous roots of grasses form a wide-spreading network that does an exceptional job holding soil in place. Creeping grasses are particularly good at this because they spread in all directions, creating a dense soil cover. Clumping grasses, though they don't spread as widely as creeping grasses, also can make an effective slope cover if you set the plants fairly close together.

Interestingly, the same root systems that make grasses beneficial for erosion control help them cope with the dry conditions that most slopes offer. Even on gentle slopes, water tends to run off the site before it can thoroughly soak into the root zone. When you plant a site with drought-tolerant grasses, however, the grasses slow the runoff, providing the extensive root systems with ready access to any water that soaks in.

Ornamental grasses are far more than a practical solution for unappealing, bedraggled slopes, however. A slope offers an ideal setting for showcasing the fountainlike habit and flowing foliage of these graceful plants. Plant the entire area with a single grass for an attractive mass planting, or cover the slope with a variety of grasses having different habits, textures, and colors for a charming tapestry effect. You also might consider combining ornamental grasses with native plants or other low-growing, drought-resistant annuals and perennials, such as hardy ice plant *(Delosperma cooperi)*, lamb's ears *(Stachys byzantina)*, stonecrop *(Sedum* spp.), and verbena *(Verbena* spp.). Whatever your approach, you'll have a great-looking, easy-care planting instead of a bothersome, high-maintenance site.

PLANTING ON A SLOPE

The toughest part of transforming a slope with grasses is preparing the soil for planting. Normally, you'd prepare a planting site either by digging or tilling the soil, or by layering organic materials on top of the soil and planting into them. Unfortunately, none of these approaches works well on an incline. It's difficult if not impossible to handle heavy equipment safely on a slope, and any loosened soil or layered organic matter will remain vulnerable to erosion until the plants fill in. That leaves you with just a few options.

• Smother the existing vegetation by covering it with plastic for a few months, then remove the plastic, trowel out individual planting holes, and mulch to cover the old, browned vegetation.

• Remove all of the existing vegetation, then cover the slope with landscape fabric or organic mulch, and set out your plants through the fabric or mulch. (If you use landscape fabric, cut Xs for individual plants, lift the flaps for planting, and then cover the fabric with an attractive mulch.)

• Build one or more low retaining walls across the slope to create level planting areas. These terraces dramatically slow the flow of water over the site, help to hold the soil in place, and are easy to plant and maintain.

• When planting grasses on a slope, set them closer together than you would on a flat site — 8 to 12 inches apart for low grasses, and about 2 feet apart for larger ones — and plant them out in a staggered, checkerboard-type pattern to create a dense, even cover. Lay soaker hoses across the slope after planting but before mulching, so you can supply water without washing away soil or mulch.

Calamagrostis foliosa

Festuca mairei

Nassella tenuissima

SLOPES

Calamagrostis foliosa
Leafy reed grass
Twelve- to 18-inch-tall, semi-evergreen clumps of blue-green foliage; flowers are slender, dense, arching, golden brown panicles held atop 24- to 30-inch-tall stems through summer. Full sun to light shade; average, well-drained soil. *Zones 7 or 8 to 9*

Carex siderosticha '**Variegata**'
Variegated broad-leaved sedge
Spreading, 1-foot-tall carpets of relatively broad, medium green leaves with white edges and white-streaked centers, tan in winter; new shoots may be tinged with pink; midsummer flowers are brownish black spikes, not especially showy. Partial shade; moist, fertile, humus-rich soil. *Zones 6 to 9*

Festuca mairei
Atlas fescue
Dense, 2-foot-tall mounds of arching, grayish green leaves that are evergreen in mild climates; narrow greenish panicles atop 3-foot-tall stems in late spring to early summer. Full sun; average to moist but well-drained, fertile soil. *Zones 5 or 6 to 10*

Leymus racemosus
Giant blue wild rye
Also known as *Elymus racemosus;* fast-spreading, rhizomatous grass with 2-foot-tall, arching, blue-green leaves; deciduous in cold climates; flowers are narrow, bluish green spikes appearing sporadically through summer atop 3- to 4-foot-tall stems. Full sun to light shade; adaptable, drought tolerant. *Zones 4 to 10*

Nassella tenuissima
Mexican feather grass
Also known as *Stipa tenuissima;* dense, 18-inch-tall fountains of fine, bright green, arching leaves, evergreen in cool climates but tend to go summer-dormant in warm climates; silky, greenish to silvery flowers appear at the top in late spring to early summer. Full sun to light shade; average, well-drained soil, highly drought tolerant. *Zones 6 or 7 to 10*

CONTROLLED ABANDON

Usually dry and frequently eroded, sloping sites are a challenge for any gardener. Still, challenge often motivates our best efforts. In this Lafayette, California, garden designed by Ron Lutsko, a slope is cloaked in an array of perennials and grasses ideally suited for parched, poor soil.

The focal point of this combination is leafy reed grass *(Calamagrostis foliosa)*, a compact species that thrives in warm climates. In a cooler area (north of Zone 8), a cultivar of large blue fescue *(Festuca amethystina)* might be a good alternative.

Though the flowers aren't quite as showy, when you consider the color of its foliage, that's not a significant drawback. Another low-growing, mounding option for gardens in Zones 6 to 9 is green-leaved, fluffy-flowered 'Little Bunny' fountain grass *(Pennisetum alopecuroides* 'Little Bunny') or its slightly shorter variegated counterpart 'Little Honey'.

Combining grasses with herbs on a slope is unexpected but perfectly natural. Many herbs demand good drainage, making them ideal candidates for sharing this site.

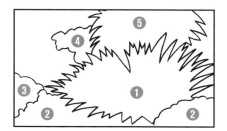

1. *Calamagrostis foliosa,* leafy reed grass
2. *Santolina virens,* lavender cotton
3. *Lavandula* sp., lavender
4. *Euphorbia* sp., spurge
5. *Deschampia cespitosa,* tufted hair grass

CREATING PRIVACY

A screen and boundary planting of ornamental grasses is an ideal way to define your property line, providing not only visual privacy, but a sound barrier as well. Grasses are equally welcome growing around a pool or patio area, or creating an attractive, fast-growing screen to block a view of your neighbor's utility area.

Variegated pampas grass (Cortaderia selloana) flourishes at the edge of a California backyard pond.

Tall-growing ornamental grasses are a good alternative if a traditional hedge is out of your price range or too large for your needs, and if you want a quick landscape fix that requires minimal maintenance. They also make excellent shrub substitutes in areas with cold winters, because they're incredibly resilient and not prone to permanent damage from heavy snowfall, ice accumulation, or even snow-removal equipment. In late winter (or earlier if your grass plantings start to look battered), simply cut them back a few inches from the ground, and you'll soon have fresh new growth to enjoy during spring.

Unlike shrubs, grasses don't provide dense, twiggy growth that discourages people and animals from crashing through. But if a physical barrier is what you need, sharp-edged grasses, such as miscanthus or pampas grass (Cortaderia selloana), can be quite unpleasant for yard crashers of all sizes. Grasses as screens and hedges offer one added benefit you won't find with closely clipped woody hedges: a soft rustling sound that does a surprisingly good job blocking background noise from the street and neighbors.

Compared to hedges, fast-growing grasses provide almost instantaneous screening. In just a few months, warm-season grasses, such as ravenna grass (Saccharum ravennae), can grow from 8 to 10 feet tall, or higher. They're dramatic as boundary plantings and make stunning accents around patios, decks, terraces, and pools. Tall grasses provide privacy when you need it most — during warm summer days and nights — but don't close you in during winter.

Grasses can also be used as temporary screening until your permanent hedges fill in. (Even the largest grasses don't provide much screening during winter, and virtually none is provided during the two to three months they require to reach a good height after their late winter trim.) Make more out of your screening by pairing the grasses with Joe Pye weed (Eupatorium maculatum), tree tobacco (Nicotiana glauca), and other

A WORD FOR THE WISE

When choosing grasses for boundary plantings, think twice before selecting species that spread by creeping roots, such as giant reed (Arundo donax) and running bamboos. Your neighbors won't appreciate having your grasses invading their yards, and that's almost inevitable unless you install sturdy metal or concrete root barriers. Considering the effort and expense that involves, you'd probably be better off installing a simple fence or traditional hedge instead.

tall annuals and perennials. Or, tuck in some summer-flowering shrubs, such as butterfly bush (*Buddleia* spp.) and chastetree *(Vitex agnus-castus)*. Each spring, cut these mixed plantings back severely (the annuals to the ground, the grasses and other perennials several inches above the ground, and the shrubs to a framework that's a foot or two tall and wide). This simple trimming is faster and easier than maintaining a closely clipped formal hedge.

Set tall-growing grasses fairly close together (30 to 36 inches apart) for the best screening in the least amount of time. If you can't find or afford to buy all the grasses you'd like at one time, buy as many of the biggest plants you can find, plant them out, then lift and divide them each spring until you fill the area. Use tall-growing annuals to provide supplemental screening in the meantime.

ABOVE: Providing a living privacy fence, *Viburnum plicatum* and 'Karl Foerster' feather reed grass (*Calamagrostis* x *acutiflora* 'Karl Foerster') also make a serene backdrop for lower-growing perennials *Nepeta* and *Kniphofia.*

LEFT: Russian sage *(Perovskia atriplicifolia)* and purple coneflower *(Echinacea purpurea)* make a dynamic color statement with feather reed grass.

Panicum virgatum

Saccharum ravennae

Arundo donax 'Variegata'

BOUNDARIES AND SCREENS

Arundo donax 'Variegata'
Giant reed
Spreading, 10- to 25-foot-tall thickets of stout, upright stems bearing green to grayish green leaves that are evergreen in mildwinter areas but turn tan at the first hard frost in cold-winter areas; large pinkish to silvery panicles in late summer to early fall. 'Variegata' has creamy white stripes that turn yellowish in warm weather. Full sun; thrives in moist, fertile soil, but adaptable. *Zones 6 to 10*

Miscanthus 'Giganteus'
Giant miscanthus
Often sold as *Miscanthus floridulus*; upright, spreading, 8- to 12-foot-tall clumps of long, arching, medium green leaves, turning reddish or purplish red in fall, then tan; late summer to early fall flowers atop 10- to 15-foot-tall stems are whisklike tassels that are reddish-tinged tan, then silvery; may not bloom in cool or short-season areas. Full sun; average to moist, well-drained, fertile soil. *Zones 4 or 5 to 9*

Panicum virgatum
Switch grass
Three- to 6-foot-tall clumps of mostly upright, green to gray-green leaves that usually turn yellow in fall; mid- to late summer flowers bloom atop 4- to 8-foot-tall stems. 'Dallas Blues' is a striking 4-foot-tall selection with relatively broad, powder blue leaves. Full sun to light shade; tolerates dry to wet soil. *Zones 4 or 5 to 9*

Saccharum contortum
Bent-awn plume grass
Also known as *Erianthus contortus*; 2-foottall clumps of upright-to-arching, green to bluish green foliage, purplish or reddish in fall; narrow, red- to purple-brown panicles in early fall on 6- to 8-foot-tall, upright stems. Full sun; moist to dry, well-drained soil. *Zones 6 or 7 to 9*

Saccharum ravennae
Hardy pampas grass, ravenna grass
Also known as *Erianthus ravennae*; 4- to 5-foot-tall clumps of arching, gray-green leaves turn orange, red-brown, or purple in fall, tan in winter; 1- to 2-foot-long, purpletinged silver plumes on 8- to 14-foot-tall, upright stems late summer to early fall, into winter; bloom undependable in cool areas. Full sun; drought tolerant but prefers evenly moist, fertile, well-drained soil. *Zones 6 to 10*

A Living Fence

In a spot where a traditional hedge isn't ideal, a row of tall ornamental grasses might be just what you need. Feather reed grass (*Calamagrostis* x *acutiflora* 'Karl Foerster') is a fabulous choice for an effective but still neighbor-friendly summer and fall screen. It reaches its full height by midsummer — many weeks earlier than most warm-season grasses. The feathery flowers top out just above eye level, tall enough to supply screening without the permanence or expense of a fence.

A boundary or screen planting is commonly a single line of like plants, but it can also serve as a backdrop for a border. This boundary to the property of Mary and Lew Reid, Sebastopol, California, is prefaced with a variety of massed grasses: arching Mexican feather grass *(Nassella tenuissima)*, mounding tufted hair grass *(Deschampsia cespitosa)*, and spiky deer grass *(Muhlenbergia rigens)*. A more typical flowering border would also look lovely against a grass screen. It's a good idea to leave a narrow path between the taller grasses and the border in front, so you can reach all parts of the planting for easy maintenance.

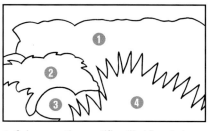

1. *Calamagrostis* x *acutiflora* 'Karl Foerster', 'Karl Foerster' feather reed grass

2. *Nassella tenuissima,* Mexican feather grass

3. *Deschampsia cespitosa,* tufted hair grass

4. *Muhlenbergia rigens,* deer grass

COVERING THE GROUND

Many ornamental grasses have dwarf forms that make extremely attractive ground covers. They provide quick cover and year-round interest, requiring just a single annual trim. Ideal on hard-to-mow slopes, these grasses are also effective around the base of trees and shrubs, where weeding and trimming are difficult.

Neat mounds of oriental fountain grass *(Pennisetum orientale)* bear pink flowers that are especially striking when lit by the sun.

Lawn grasses are the most widely grown group of ground-cover plants. And little wonder: it's easy to buy a bag of grass seed or some sprigs to get a decent patch of turf started. After that, though, the work never ends. To keep the grass vigorous enough to crowd out weeds, you'll need to fertilize it regularly, and probably water it, too. Unfortunately, all that health and vigor means that you'll have to mow it every few days to keep it looking tidy.

With ornamental grasses, you can enjoy most of the benefits of lawn grasses, but without all the feeding, watering, and mowing. Most ornamental grasses aren't tough enough to withstand the heavy foot traffic that turf grasses endure, but they *can* be nearly as easy to start, and they *can* create a low, green carpet that from a distance gives the illusion of a conventional lawn. These pseudo-lawns might not be formal enough for a front yard, but they're just the thing for lesser-used parts of the landscape, such as the side yard. Set a series of stepping-stones through the area, and you'll have easy access through the planting without any need to tread on the delicate grasses. This is also a place to create some delightful interest early in the season by interplanting the grasses with small spring bulbs, such as reticulated irises *(Iris reticulata)* and crocuses.

Ornamental grasses are more than just lawn substitutes, of course; they're also beautiful plants in their own right. You might want to use only green foliage in your ground cover, but you can easily incorporate a different texture, such as the gracefully arching foliage of Hakone grass *(Hakonechloa macra)*. Instead of creating a level carpet, and for a totally different look, consider a ground-cover planting with a species that has a distinctly mounding form, such as prairie dropseed *(Sporobolus heterolepis)*.

Looking for something *really* different? Try an ornamental grass with a foliage color other than green. Imagine the eye-catching effect of an area filled with the bright blue foliage of blue oat grass *(Helictotrichon sempervirens)*, for example, or a cranberry-red mass of Japanese blood grass *(Imperata cylindrica* var. *koenigii* 'Red Baron'). And don't overlook the wide variety of grasses with great-looking flowers. Ground-cover plantings are a perfect way to enjoy species with delicate blooms, such as perennial quaking

grass *(Briza media)*. A single clump of these grasses can easily get lost among other plants, but a mass planting offers considerably more interest and opportunity for close inspection.

Traditional ground-cover plantings typically use plants that are about 2 feet tall or less. If you're hoping for a lawn-like effect, restrict yourself to the lowest-growing species you can find, such as blue fescue *(Festuca glauca)*. In the 6- to 24-inch height range, you have a much wider variety of grasses from which to choose, especially if you don't mind an additional foot or so of growth when they flower.

A muted and varied tapestry of Mexican feather grass *(Nassella tenuissima)*, purple fountain grass *(Pennisetum setaceum* 'Rubrum'), and oriental fountain grass *(Pennisetum orientale)* grows near a mass planting of switch grass *(Panicum virgatum)*.

If ground cover is what you want, this is one time that grasses with creeping roots and self-sowing tendencies are truly welcome. In a ground-cover planting, the idea is to fill space, and new shoots and volunteer seedlings simply help further that cause. Of course, being an ecologically responsible gardener, you'll want to avoid using grasses that are considered serious weed problems in your area so you're not encouraging plants that are destructive to native habitats.

Creeping grasses tend to form fairly uniform carpets on their own, no matter how you space them; it does take them longer to fill in when more widely spaced, however. If you choose creeping grasses for your ground-cover, be sure to surround the outer edge of the planting area with an edging strip or root barrier. Mowing regularly around the creepers will do a fair job of containing them, but lawn grasses might still sneak in and create a messy-looking edge to your planting. A mowing strip keeps the whole mass looking neat and tidy.

Clumping grasses provide you with several planting options. If you use a spacing approximately equal to the plant's width (if the clumps reach 2 feet across, for example, then set them 2 feet apart), each plant will maintain its individual form, mingling only at the leaf tips. Closer spacings will yield a more uniform look, better weed-smothering effect, and faster coverage, but be forewarned that crowding the plants too closely — at a spacing less than half of their normal width — can lead to disease problems due to poor air circulation.

Inviting cool whites and gray-greens, including snowy woodrush *(Luzula nivea)* and *Eryngium* sp., line this pathway under a row of fruit trees.

Keep in mind that even drought-tolerant grasses require some supplemental water during their first year, so consider laying soaker hoses through the area after planting to make future watering a snap. Remove the hoses after the first season, or leave them in place just in case you choose to provide supplemental water in following years.

And, of course, don't forget to mulch. By their second or third year, your grasses will have filled in enough to create a dense, weed-suppressing cover. In the meantime, though, a 1- to 2-inch layer of mulch will shade the soil enough to prevent most weed seeds from sprouting, and those that do come up will be easier to pull. Once established, ground-cover grasses benefit from a light compost mulch every year or two, to help maintain soil organic matter.

Warm-season grasses, such as fountain grass *(Pennisetum alopecuroides)*, benefit from a trim in late winter or early spring to remove dead foliage and seed heads. A string trimmer makes quick work of tending to even a large-scale ground-cover grass planting. (Refer to page 26 for an illustration of an easy way to cut tall grasses back.) Sedges and cool-season grasses may require just a light trim or no grooming at all.

CONSIDER YOUR OPTIONS

Compared to the cost of turf grass seed or sprigs, a ground-cover planting can seem a bit pricey. One way to minimize the cost is to buy a few plants, grow them, and then divide them every year or two. Another option is to seek out a supplier who will sell you "plugs." These plants are small, and you'll probably have to buy several dozen or more at one time, but the price per plant will be significantly less than that of individually potted, nursery-size specimens, and they'll fill in quickly.

Yet another way to fill your garden with grasses is to start them yourself from seed. Seed-grown plants can be somewhat variable, but if you don't mind that they may be a good option for you. If you want a more uniform look, vegetatively propagated cultivars are the better choice.

The most difficult part of growing ornamental grasses from seed can be finding a seed source. You'll probably need to look in catalogs specializing in unusual seeds to find more than the two or three most common species. Once you have the seed, start the plants indoors as you would other perennials, or sow the seed directly into prepared soil in early spring, just as you would turf grass seed.

The list that follows highlights some handsome perennial grasses that are generally easy to grow from seed and suitable for use as groundcovers and mass plantings.

Andropogon spp. (andropogons)
Bouteloua spp. (grama grasses)
Briza media (perennial quaking grass)
Chasmanthium latifolium (wild oats)
Deschampsia spp. (hair grasses)
Eragrostis spp. (love grasses)
Festuca spp. (fescues)
Helictotrichon sempervirens (blue oat grass)

Koeleria spp. (hair grasses)
Nassella tenuissima (Mexican feather grass)
Pennisetum spp. (fountain grasses)
Schizachyrium scoparium (little bluestem)
Sporobolus heterolepis (prairie dropseed)

Deschampsia cespitosa

Deschampsia flexuosa 'Aurea'

Sporobolus heterolepis

GREAT GROUND COVERS

Deschampsia cespitosa
Tufted hair grass

Two- to 3-foot-tall, often-evergreen clumps of spiky to arching, deep green foliage; airy panicles of yellowish green spikelets atop 3- to 5-foot-tall stems in summer. *Deschampsia flexuosa* 'Aurea' has yellow-green foliage. Partial shade; evenly moist, well-drained, humus-rich soil. *Zones 4 to 9*

Eragrostis curvula
Weeping love grass

Dense, 2-foot-tall mounds of fine, dark green leaves with reddish or yellowish tints in fall; evergreen in mild climates; gracefully arching, 2- to 3-foot-tall stems bear open, silvery purple panicles in mid- to late-summer. Full sun; average, well-drained soil; drought-tolerant when established. *Zones 7 to 10*

Sasa veitchii
Silver-edge bamboo

Spreading masses of slender, upright stems about 3 feet tall; broad leaves are dark green in summer, with broad cream-colored edges in fall and winter (sometimes all light tan in extreme cold). Partial shade; prefers evenly moist soil but tolerates dry conditions. *Zones 6 or 7 to 10*

Sesleria caerulea
Blue moor grass

Compact, 6- to 12-inch-tall clumps of narrow, twisted leaves that are dark green on top and silver blue underneath; evergreen where mild; short, spikelike panicles on 20-inch stems in spring, purplish brown, turning greenish white, then tan. Full sun to light shade; drought tolerant, but prefers moist, well-drained, fertile soil. *Zones 5 to 9*

Sporobolus heterolepis
Prairie dropseed

Dense, 18- to 24-inch-tall mounds of gracefully arching, slender, glossy, green leaves that turn golden or orange in fall, coppery brown in winter; late summer to early fall flowers are aromatic, airy, silvery panicles on 30- to 36-inch-tall stems. Full sun to light shade; tolerates heat and drought. *Zones 4 to 8*

LIVELY GROUND COVERS

Not so long ago, gardeners who wanted ground covers for shade had to choose one of the all-too-predictable "big three": English ivy *(Hedera helix)*, common periwinkle *(Vinca minor)*, and Japanese pachysandra *(Pachysandra terminalis)*. Today, ground covers aren't merely expanses of evergreen foliage used to fill space under trees and shrubs. And they needn't be confined to the shade, either; ground covers can replace lawn grasses in sunny spots to provide ever-changing seasonal interest and eliminate weekly mowing.

Ornamental grasses — both the sunlovers and those made for the shade — are excellent options for mass plantings that are attractive as well as practical. Most, like the Oriental fountain grass *(Pennisetum orientale)* used in this eye-catching design by Richard McPherson in Los Altos, California, need only a yearly trim.

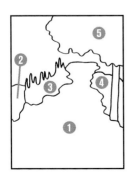

1. *Pennisetum orientale,* oriental fountain grass

2. *Nepeta* sp., catmint

3. *Lavandula* sp., lavender

4. *Hemerocallis* sp., daylilies

5. *Liriodendron tulipifera,* tulip tree

EASY DOES IT

You'll often hear ornamental grasses touted as being low-maintenance, and as a group, they do tend to require less care than traditional garden plants. But when you start getting to know individual grasses, you'll quickly discover that some need even less attention than others.

CHOOSING LOW-MAINTENANCE GRASSES

If your goal is a grass planting that requires little to no maintenance, the ideal grass for you will possess some or all of the following characteristics:

- Minimal or no self-sowing
- Clumping or slow-spreading habit
- Seldom requires division
- Minimal need for supplemental watering
- Not especially prone to pests or diseases
- Sturdy stems that don't require staking
- No need for winter protection in your climate

Not many grasses have all of these traits, but there are a few. If you're willing to compromise on one or more of the desirable traits, many more options will be available to you. Simply follow the care suggestions in this section, and you can create a great-looking, easy-care planting.

RIGHT: Pampas grasses are among the most dramatically beautiful and easy-care ornamental grasses. Growing here are both tall (*Cortaderia selloana* 'Aureolineata') and dwarf ('Pumila') forms.

What makes one grass higher maintenance than another? That depends a good deal on your particular likes and dislikes. If you find weeding to be a peaceful, contemplative activity, then a self-sowing grass may be just the thing for you. On the other hand, if you simply detest weeding, you'll want to avoid grasses that tend to self-sow; otherwise, be prepared to take on the extra chore of trimming off the flower heads before the seeds ripen.

Following the current trend toward a less formal, more natural planting style, you can combine ornamental grasses with carefully chosen flowering perennials to create gardens that mimic the randomness and repetition of natural environments, such as prairies, but on a more modest scale.

A meadow planting is an obvious way to enjoy grasses in a natural-looking setting, but these plantings aren't for everyone. You may recognize the beauty of the individual grasses and appreciate the ecological benefits of their diversity, but your neighbors may see only a patch of unmown weeds. By combining similar plants into drifts and using some recognizable (but still low-maintenance) flowering perennials with the grasses, you can create a diverse and easy-care planting that others not "in the know" will enjoy.

The most critical first step in choosing a low-maintenance grass is accurately assessing the growing conditions your site has to offer. Planting a moisture-loving grass in poor sandy soil, or a sun-lover in a shady site, will lead to weak, problem-prone growth that's far more bother than it's worth. A grass that is well suited to your climate, exposure, soil, and natural rainfall patterns, on the

other hand, will grow and thrive with minimal effort on your part.

If you want to grow a grass that needs more moisture than you get by rainfall, consider installing a soaker hose or drip irrigation system. Setting up the system and remembering to use it takes more effort than not watering at all, but it does take much less time than watering by hand. Maintaining a layer of mulch on the soil helps reduce both watering and weeding chores, because it slows water loss due to evaporation and prevents weed seeds from getting the light they require to sprout.

To reduce the need for frequent division, avoid overwatering, keep fertilizing to a minimum, and give your grasses enough room to grow without being crowded by their companions.

Bursts of fireworks identify leafy reed grass *(Calamagrostis foliosa)*, here sharing the stage with an exuberant garden that also features *Santolina* and lavender.

Miscanthus sinensis 'Strictus'

Miscanthus transmorrisonensis

Muhlenbergia rigens

LOW MAINTENANCE

Calamagrostis brachytricha
Korean feather reed grass

Two-foot-tall clumps of upright to arching, glossy green leaves that turn yellowish in fall; feathery, silvery pink plumes appear atop 4-foot-tall stems in late summer and early fall, aging to tan and lasting into winter. Full sun (if soil is moist) to partial shade; adaptable. *Zones 5 to 9*

Hakonechloa macra
Hakone grass

Loose, slowly expanding, 1- to 2-foot-tall mounds of arching, glossy green leaves that turn copper-colored in fall; airy greenish to tan panicles in late summer and early fall, not especially showy. Can take sun if moist, but generally best in partial shade; evenly moist, well-drained, humus-rich soil. *Zones 5 to 9*

Miscanthus sinensis 'Strictus'
Porcupine grass

Upright, 4- to 6-foot-tall clumps of green leaves with horizontal light yellow bands, turning tan throughout by winter; branched, reddish brown flower clusters in early fall atop 6- to 8-foot-tall stems. Much less likely to need staking than the similarly variegated 'Zebrinus'. Full sun to light shade; average to evenly moist soil. *Zones 5 to 9*

Miscanthus transmorrisonensis
Evergreen miscanthus

Dense, 3- to 4-foot-tall clumps of arching, narrow green leaves that are evergreen into Zone 7; branched, reddish brown flower clusters, turning tan, held well above the foliage on 4- to 6-foot-tall stems, appearing as early as late spring in mild climates and mid- to late-summer in cooler zones. Full sun to light shade; adaptable but prefers evenly moist, fertile soil. *Zones 6 or 7 to 10*

Muhlenbergia rigens
Deer grass

Two- to 3-foot-tall, semi-evergreen clumps of spiky, grayish green leaves; slender, silvery flower panicles appear in midsummer, then turn tan and last well into winter. Full sun to light shade; prefers fertile, moist, well-drained soil but has good drought tolerance once established. *Zones 7 to 10*

AN EASY-CARE GARDEN

How much maintenance time would you be willing to give to have a pretty planting like this one at Kistler Winery in Forestville, California, in your own yard? How about just an hour or two per year? Ornamental grasses are one of the best investments you can make: they look great for much of the season and require only a few minutes of grooming and an annual trim in return.

This garden features the easy-care perennials pink twinspur (*Diascia* sp.) and pink-and-white fleabane *(Erigeron karvinskianus)*. Well-suited to rock gardens and other well-drained sites, both pair perfectly with the blue oat grass *(Helictotrichon sempervirens)* and evergreen miscanthus *(Miscanthus transmorrisonensis)* for a marvelous low-maintenance planting. *Diascia* is hardy only in Zones 8 and 9. In cooler areas you can successfully grow this plant as an annual, or, if you prefer, use a perennial like gaura, which blooms throughout most of the season. White gaura *(Gaura lindheimeri)* is always attractive, but to retain the pink-and-blue color scheme, try the deep pink 'Siskiyou Pink'.

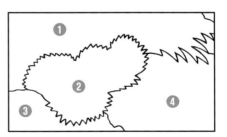

1. *Miscanthus transmorrisonensis*, evergreen miscanthus
2. *Helictotrichon sempervirens*, blue oat grass
3. *Diascia* sp., pink twinspur
4. *Erigeron karvinskianus*, fleabane

USDA HARDINESS ZONE MAP

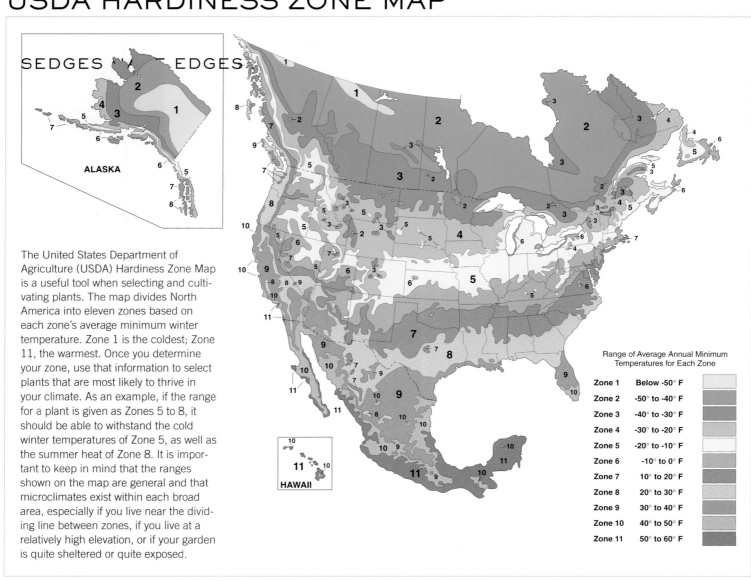

SEDGES AND EDGES

ALASKA

HAWAII

The United States Department of Agriculture (USDA) Hardiness Zone Map is a useful tool when selecting and cultivating plants. The map divides North America into eleven zones based on each zone's average minimum winter temperature. Zone 1 is the coldest; Zone 11, the warmest. Once you determine your zone, use that information to select plants that are most likely to thrive in your climate. As an example, if the range for a plant is given as Zones 5 to 8, it should be able to withstand the cold winter temperatures of Zone 5, as well as the summer heat of Zone 8. It is important to keep in mind that the ranges shown on the map are general and that microclimates exist within each broad area, especially if you live near the dividing line between zones, if you live at a relatively high elevation, or if your garden is quite sheltered or quite exposed.

Range of Average Annual Minimum Temperatures for Each Zone

Zone 1	Below -50° F
Zone 2	-50° to -40° F
Zone 3	-40° to -30° F
Zone 4	-30° to -20° F
Zone 5	-20° to -10° F
Zone 6	-10° to 0° F
Zone 7	10° to 20° F
Zone 8	20° to 30° F
Zone 9	30° to 40° F
Zone 10	40° to 50° F
Zone 11	50° to 60° F

The following pages offer lists of grasses that are especially useful for specific purposes, including color combinations, particular sites in the landscape, and problem solving. These lists supplement the descriptions and photos included on the Designer's Choice pages throughout the text of this book. Grasses described in the text for each section are highlighted with an asterisk (*).

GREAT GRASSES FOR EVERY NEED

GOLD AND BRONZE GRASSES

Acorus gramineus 'Ogon'

Alopecurus pratensis 'Variegatus'

Bromus inermis 'Skinner's Gold'

Carex comans 'Bronze' *

Carex elata 'Aurea' *

Deschampsia flexuosa 'Aurea' *

Festuca glauca 'Golden Toupee'

Hakonechloa macra 'Aureola' *

Liriope muscari 'PeeDee Ingot' *

Luzula sylvatica 'Aurea'

Milium effusum 'Aureum'

Pleioblastus viridistriatus *

BLUE AND GRAY GRASSES

Carex flacca

Festuca amethystina 'Superba'

Festuca glauca *

Festuca idahoensis 'Siskiyou Blue'

Helictotrichon sempervirens *

Juncus patens *

Koeleria glauca *

Leymus condensatus 'Canyon Prince'

Leymus racemosus

Panicum virgatum 'Cloud Nine' *

Panicum virgatum 'Dallas Blues'

Schizachyrium scoparium 'The Blues' *

Sorghastrum nutans 'Sioux Blue' *

DARK-LEAVED GRASSES

Imperata cylindrica
    var. *koenigii* 'Red Baron' *

Ophiopogon planiscapus 'Nigrescens'

Panicum virgatum 'Shenandoah'

Pennisetum 'Burgundy Giant' *

Pennisetum setaceum 'Rubrum' *

Phormium tenax 'Rubrum'

Saccharum officinarum 'Pele's Smoke' *

Uncinia rubra *

VARIEGATED GRASSES

Acorus gramineus 'Ogon' *

Alopecurus pratensis 'Variegatus'

Arrhenatherum elatius
    ssp. *bulbosum* 'Variegatum'

Arundo donax 'Variegata'

Calamagrostis x *acutiflora* 'Overdam'

Carex morrowii 'Variegata' *

Carex phyllocephala 'Sparkler' *

Cortaderia selloana 'Silver Comet'

Deschampsia cespitosa

Glyceria maxima 'Variegata'

Hakonechloa macra 'Aureola'

Miscanthus sinensis 'Strictus' *

Miscanthus sinensis
    var. *condensatus* 'Cosmopolitan' *

Phalaris arundinacea 'Dwarf Garters' *

Pleioblastus viridistriatus

Setaria palmifolia 'Variegata'

Phormium 'Sea Jade'

Miscanthus spp. and *Pennisetum* spp.

WORKING WITH COLOR

Alopecurus pratensis 'Variegatus' *

Carex elata 'Aurea' *

Elegia capensis

Eragrostis spectabilis *

Festuca amethystina 'Superba'

Imperata cylindrica
  var. *koenigii* 'Red Baron' *

Panicum virgatum 'Shenandoah'

Pennisetum alopecuroides 'Moudry' *

Pennisetum setaceum 'Rubrum' *

Phormium tenax *

Schizachyrium scoparium 'The Blues' *

Themeda japonica *

FRONT YARDS

Calamagrostis x *acutiflora* 'Karl Foerster' *

Calamagrostis brachytricha

Carex dolichostachya 'Kaga Nishiki'

Cortaderia selloana 'Pumila' *

Elymus magellanicus

Festuca glauca 'Elijah Blue' *

Hakonechloa macra 'Aureola'

Helictotrichon sempervirens

Imperata cylindrica
  var. *koenigii* 'Red Baron' *

Miscanthus sinensis 'Adagio' *

Molinia caerulea 'Variegata'

Pennisetum alopecuroides 'Hameln' *

Stipa spp.

BEDS AND BORDERS

Achnatherum calamagrostis

Arrhenatherum elatius
  ssp. *bulbosum* 'Variegatum'

Calamagrostis x *acutiflora* 'Overdam'

Carex spp., including *Carex*
  dolichostachya 'Kaga Nishiki' *

Cortaderia selloana 'Pumila'

Elymus magellanicus *

Festuca glauca

Festuca idahoensis 'Siskiyou Blue' *

Hakonechloa macra 'Aureola'

Helictotrichon sempervirens

Milium effusum 'Aureum'

Miscanthus sinensis 'Morning Light'

Miscanthus sinensis 'Gracillimus' *

Molinia caerulea 'Variegata'

Pennisetum alopecuroides

Stipa spp.

ROSE COMPANIONS

Carex oshimensis 'Evergold' *

Cortaderia spp., including
  C. selloana 'Monvin' *

Cymbopogon citratus *

Festuca amethystina 'Superba' *

Miscanthus sinensis 'Variegatus' *

Panicum virgatum 'Heavy Metal'

PATHS AND WALKWAYS

Briza media

Carex morrowii 'Variegata'

Carex muskingumensis 'Oehme'

Carex tumulicola *

Deschampsia cespitosa 'Fairy's Joke' *

Festuca amethystina *

Hakonechloa macra

Lagurus ovatus *

Luzula spp., including *L. sylvatica* *

Ophiopogon spp.

Pennisetum spp.

Phalaris arundinacea 'Dwarf Garters'

Sporobolus heterolepis

POTS AND PLANTERS

Bromus inermis 'Skinner's Gold' *

Carex phyllocephala 'Sparkler'

Chasmanthium latifolium

Cyperus papyrus *

Imperata cylindrica var. *koenigii* 'Red Baron'

Isolepis cernua *

Juncus effusus 'Spiralis'

Leymus arenarius *

Miscanthus sinensis

Muhlenbergia dumosa

Nassella tenuissima

Ophiopogon planiscapus 'Nigrescens' *

Pennisetum spp.

Phormium cookianum 'Flamingo'

Pleioblastus viridistriatus *

Saccharum officinale 'Pele's Smoke'

Stenotaphrum secundatum 'Variegatum'

ACCENT PLANTS

Carex elata 'Aurea'

Carex muskingumensis 'Oehme' *

Cortaderia selloana *

Elegia capensis *

Fargesia nitida *

Helictotrichon sempervirens

Miscanthus sinensis 'Gracillimus'

Molinia caerulea subsp. *arundinacea* 'Skyracer'

Muhlenbergia spp.

Panicum virgatum 'Heavy Metal' *

Pennisetum setaceum 'Rubrum'

Phyllostachys nigra

Saccharum ravennae

Spodiopogon sibiricus

Stipa gigantea *

Miscanthus sinensis 'Silberfeder'

SMALL SPACES

Acorus gramineus 'Pusillus' *

Arrhenatherum elatius
  var. *bulbosum* 'Variegatum'

Carex 'The Beatles'

Carex conica 'Snowline' *

Carex muskingumensis 'Oehme'

Festuca glauca

Hakonechloa macra 'Aureola'

Imperata cylindrica
  var. *koenigii* 'Red Baron'

Juncus effusus 'Spiralis'

Luzula spp.

Molinia caerulea 'Variegata' *

Ophiopogon japonicus 'Nana' *

Pennisetum alopecuroides 'Little Bunny' *

Sesleria spp.

WATER GARDENS

Acorus spp.

Arundo donax

Carex elata 'Aurea'

Cyperus papyrus

Eriophorum spp.

Equisetum hyemale *

Glyceria maxima 'Variegata' *

Isolepis cernua

Juncus spp., including *Juncus effusus*
  'Unicorn' *

Schoenoplectus lacustris
  ssp. *tabernaemontani* 'Zebrinus' *

Scirpus spp.

Spartina pectinata

Typha latifolia 'Variegata' *

FALL COLOR

Andropogon spp. *

Anemanthele lessoniana *

Bouteloua curtipendula

Miscanthus 'Purpurascens'

Miscanthus sinensis *

Molinia caerulea ssp. *arundinacea* *

Panicum virgatum *

Pennisetum alopecuroides

Saccharum contortum

Schizachyrium scoparium

Sorghastrum nutans

Spartina pectinata

Spodiopogon sibiricus *

Themeda japonica

Hot, Dry Sites

Achnatherum hymenoides *

Andropogon ternarius

Bouteloua gracilis *

Eragrostis curvula

Festuca glauca

Helictotrichon sempervirens

Koeleria macrantha

Muhlenbergia capillaris *

Schizachyrium scoparium *

Sorghastrum nutans *

Sporobolus heterolepis

Shade-Lovers

Arrhenatherum elatius
   ssp. *bulbosum* 'Variegatum' *

Carex spp., including *C. siderosticha*
   'Variegata' *

Chasmanthium latifolium *

Deschampsia flexuosa *

Hakonechloa macra

Hystrix patula *

Luzula nivea *

Milium effusum 'Aureum' * *

Sasa veitchii

Sesleria autumnalis

Spodiopogon sibiricus

Moisture-Lovers

Achnatherum calamagrostis

Acorus calamus *

Andropogon glomeratus

Arundo donax

Calamagrostis x *acutiflora* 'Karl Foerster'

Carex grayi *

Carex muskingumensis

Eriophorum angustifolium *

Juncus effusus, including 'Carman's
   Japanese' *

Miscanthus sinensis

Phalaris arundinacea 'Picta' *

Spartina pectinata 'Aureomarginata' *

Typha spp. (cattails)

Boundaries and Screens

Andropogon gerardii

Arundo donax *

Calamagrostis x *acutiflora* 'Karl Foerster'

Cortaderia selloana

Fargesia spp.

Miscanthus 'Giganteus' *

Miscanthus transmorrisonensis

Panicum virgatum 'Dallas Blues' *

Phyllostachys nigra

Saccharum contortum *

Saccharum ravennae *

Sorghastrum nutans 'Sioux Blue'

Sporobolus heterolepis

SLOPES

Calamagrostis foliosa *
Carex flagellifera
Carex siderosticha 'Variegata' *
Chasmanthium latifolium
Eragrostis curvula *
Festuca glauca
Festuca mairei *
Hakonechloa macra
Leymus arenarius
Leymus racemosus *
Muhlenbergia rigens (deer grass)
Nassella tenuissima *
Pennisetum spp.
Phalaris arundinacea 'Picta'
Pleioblastus viridistriatus

GROUND COVERS

Carex flacca
Carex siderosticha 'Variegata'
Deschampsia cespitosa *
Eragrostis curvula *
Hakonechloa macra
Helictotrichon sempervirens
Imperata cylindrica
  var. *koenigii* 'Red Baron'
Leymus spp.
Luzula sylvatica
Pennisetum spp.
Phalaris arundinacea 'Picta'
Sasa veitchii *
Sesleria caerulea *
Sporobolus heterolepis *

LOW MAINTENANCE

Calamagrostis brachytricha *
Calamagrostis x *acutiflora* 'Karl Foerster'
Carex dolichostachya 'Kaga Nishiki'
Cortaderia selloana
Fargesia spp.
Hakonechloa macra *
Imperata cylindrica
  var. *koenigii* 'Red Baron'
Luzula nivea
Miscanthus sinensis 'Strictus' *
Miscanthus transmorrisonensis *
Muhlenbergia lindheimeri
Muhlenbergia rigens *
Saccharum ravennae
Sesleria spp.

Pennisetum spp.

Helictotrichon sempervirens

Cortaderia selloana 'Pumila'

GARDEN, LOCATION, AND DESIGN CREDITS

This Los Altos, California, garden designed by Richard McPherson may be my favorite. Not the most showy or colorful or dramatic, perhaps, but satisfying and comfortable to behold. Wouldn't you want to sit on a bench here and watch the birds flitting about the meadow and the larger flowering grasses dancing in the breeze? Every time I go back, I am drawn to this man-made meadow, truly the best use of grasses.

—SAXON HOLT

The photographer wishes to acknowledge the many public garden locations that welcomed him so warmly: Bob Lilly and Bellevue Botanic Garden, Seattle, Washington; Boerner Botanical Gardens, Hales Corners, Wisconsin; Chris Woods and Chanticleer Garden, Wayne, Pennsylvania; Dennis Wildnauer and Cornerstone Gardens, Germansville, Pennsylvania; Sarah Duke Gardens, Durham, North Carolina; Filoli Garden, Woodside, California; Heronswood Nursery, Kingston, Washington; Limerock Ornamental Grasses, State College, Pennsylvania; Longwood Gardens, Kennett Square, Pennsylvania; Meadowbrook Farm Nursery, Meadowbrook, Pennsylvania; Richard Hartledge and Elisabeth C. Miller Botanical Garden, Seattle, Washington; Minnesota Landscape Arboretum, Minneapolis, Minnesota; Nancy Goodwin and Montrose Garden,

Hillsborough, North Carolina; Noerenberg Park, Minnetonka, Minnesota; Tony Avent and Plant Delights Nursery, Raleigh, North Carolina; Edith Eddleman and J. C. Raulston Arboretum, Raleigh, North Carolina; Scott Arboretum, Swarthmore, Pennsylvania; Strybing Arboretum, San Francisco, California; and Western Hills Nursery, Occidental, California.

Special thanks also to Steven Antonow; Dan Boroff; Linda Cochran; Marcia Donohue; Paul and Kay Fireman; Jenny and Scott Fleming; Heidi Freestone; Keith Geller; Dr. and Mrs. Roger Greenberg; Bob Hornback (designer) and Kistler Winery, Forestville, California; Jenny Hunt; John and Glennis Jones; Ron Lutsko (designer); Richard McPherson (designer); Sharon Osmund; Michael Petrie; Suzanne Porter (designer); Roger Raiche; Gary Ratway (designer) and Matanzas Creek Winery, Santa Rosa, California; Mary and Lew Reid; Freeland Tanner (designer); and Brandon Tyson (designer). Finally, thanks Flora!

Note: Botanical nomenclature continues to evolve; the principal nomenclature reference for this book is *The Color Encyclopedia of Ornamental Grasses* by Rick Darke (Portland, Oreg.: Timber Press, 1999). Numbers set in *italics* indicate illustrations and photographs; numbers set in **boldface** refer to the Great Grasses for Every Need chart.

INDEX

OTHER STOREY TITLES YOU MIGHT ENJOY

Deckscaping
Barbara W. Ellis

Create your own outdoor sanctuary using the landscaping and planting techniques provided in this comprehensive text. Full-color photographs and illustrations throughout. 176 pages. Hardcover. ISBN 1-58017-459-0. Paperback. ISBN 1-58017-408-6.

Designing Your Gardens and Landscapes
Janet Macunovich

With this practical 12-step approach, readers learn to set goals, budget, assess a site, create a plant list, and use garden focal points to best advantage. 176 pages. Paperback. ISBN 1-58017-315-2.

Garden Stone
Barbara Pleasant

Full-color photographs and clear instructions provide readers with v isual inspiration and creative ways to use stone in the garden. 240 pages. Hardcover. ISBN 1-58017-406-X.

Herbalist's Garden
Shatoiya and Richard de la Tour

Come inside the garden gates of North America's most enchanting herb gardens and hear about their owners' gardening joys and challenges and favorite plants. 240 pages. Hardcover with jacket. ISBN 1-58017-410-8.

Landscaping Makes Cents
Frederick C. Campbell and Richard L. Dubé

A complete guide to adding substantial value and beauty to a home through careful landscape design. 176 pages. Paperback. ISBN 0-88266-948-6.

Lawn and Garden Owner's Manual
Lewis and Nancy Hill

This homeowner's ultimate landscape care and maintenance manual allows the reader to diagnose and cure lawn and garden problems, rejuvenate neglected landscaping, and maintain beautiful and healthy grounds throughout the year. 192 pages. Paperback. ISBN 1-58017-214-8.

Outdoor Water Features
Alan and Gill Bridgewater

Clear step-by-step photographs and easy-to-follow instructions make this the ideal how-to guide for readers who dream of incorporating water features in their gardens. 128 pages. Paperback. ISBN 1-58017-334-9.

The Practical Guide to Container Gardening
Susan Berry and Steve Bradley

This inspiring and beautiful book is a comprehensive reference for choosing the best containers for specific plants, planning seasonal planting schemes, and using simple planting techniques and proper plant maintenance. 160 pages. Paperback. ISBN 1-58017-329-2.

The Vegetable Gardener's Bible
Edward C. Smith

Discover the last W-O-R-D in vegetable gardening with Ed Smith's amazing system — Wide rows, Organic methods, Raised beds, and Deep soil. 320 pages. Paperback. ISBN 1-58017-212-1.

These books and other Storey Books are available at your bookstore, farm store, garden center, or directly from Storey Books, 210 MASS MoCA Way, North Adams, MA 01247 or by calling 1-800-441-5700. Or visit our Web site at www.storey.com